MOVING FOR A B

Harris Hill, the UK's leading charity and 'non-profit' recruitment specialist. As a candidate Harris Hill should be your first point of contact for Permanent, Temporary and Executive vacancies, and as a client, for the recruitment of high quality and professional personnel.

We are committed to delivering a level of excellence unrivalled in the recruitment industry to both candidates and clients alike and put service and professionalism at the forefront of all we do.

THE ATRIUM SUITE
BISHOPS PALACE HOUSE
RIVERSIDE WALK
KINGSTON UPON THAMES
SURREY KT1 1QN

TELEPHONE 020 8974 9990

FAX 020 8974 6000

EMAIL info@harrishill.co.uk

WEB www.harrishill.co.uk

harrishill
CHARITY RECRUITMENT SPECIALISTS

INVESTORS IN PEOPLE

acevo
CORPORATE MEMBER

Institute of
Fundraising
ORGANISATIONAL
MEMBER

REC
Recruitment &
Employment
Confederation

Permanent · Temporary · Executive

MOVING FOR A BRIGHTER FUTURE IN FUNDRAISING

Harris Hill, the UK's leading charity and 'non-profit' recruitment specialist. As a candidate Harris Hill should be your first point of contact for Permanent, Temporary and Executive vacancies, and as a client, for the recruitment of high quality and professional personnel.

We are committed to delivering a level of excellence unrivalled in the recruitment industry to both candidates and clients alike and put service and professionalism at the forefront of all we do.

THE ATRIUM SUITE
BISHOPS PALACE HOUSE
RIVERSIDE WALK
KINGSTON UPON THAMES
SURREY KT1 1QN

TELEPHONE 020 8974 9990

FAX 020 8974 6000

EMAIL info@harrishill.co.uk

WEB www.harrishill.co.uk

harrishill
CHARITY RECRUITMENT SPECIALISTS

INVESTORS IN PEOPLE

acevo
CORPORATE MEMBER

Institute of
Fundraising
ORGANISATIONAL
MEMBER

Recruitment &
Employment
Confederation

Permanent • Temporary • Executive

Working in Fundraising

2004–05

edited by
Liza Ramrayka

Published by Guardian Books
Guardian Books is an imprint of Guardian Newspapers Ltd

The Guardian and SocietyGuardian are trademarks of the
Guardian Media Group plc and Guardian Newspapers Ltd

A CIP record for this book is available from the
British Library

ISBN 1 84354 328 1

Distributed by Atlantic Books,
an imprint of Grove Atlantic Ltd, Ormond House,
26-27 Boswell Street, London WC1N 3JZ

Cover Design: Two Associates
Text and graphics by carrstudio www.carrstudio.co.uk

Printed and Bound by Cromwell Press Trowbridge Wiltshire

Contents

About the Institute of Fundraising 165

Directory

Glossary 190

Foreword

By Simon Burne
Chair, Institute of Fundraising

Fundraising is unique. It is the most visible face of charity in the UK and benefits from the many millions of people who give their money or time. But behind the scenes is a core of professional, dedicated full-time career fundraisers without whom these activities could not succeed.

The existence of voluntary fundraisers can make gaining recognition for fundraising as a career a difficult task. But a career it certainly is, and a modern, flexible one at that.

Many come to fundraising as a second career, bringing with them skills and experience that make them ideal fundraisers. Many school leavers and graduates find fundraising an ideal first step on the work experience ladder. Large numbers of fundraisers take career breaks, juggle to bring up a family, work from home and have flexible hours.

The wide variety of roles available makes fundraising a stimulating career choice, with exciting prospects for skills development and job progression. And of course, raising funds to make a difference to a wide range of causes and issues brings real job satisfaction.

This unique combination makes fundraising a rewarding and cutting edge career for the 21st century.

Fundraising is experiencing real growth. New charities are established each year while existing ones are constantly looking for new ways to fund their work. There are also increased demands for fundraisers in education (both schools and universities), the arts and in health. Yet there is a real shortage of individuals with the skills necessary to fill these roles.

This guide is aimed principally at those considering or investigating the opportunities for a career in fundraising. However, it will be of equal interest to the many thousands who are already working in this sector and want to further develop their career.

The guide draws on the experience and skills of many of the 4,000 individual members of the Institute of Fundraising. The Institute provides its members with support through training, networking and information to help them become better fundraisers. With a very strong and active network across the whole of the UK we allow fundraisers to share knowledge and best practice no matter where they are based.

In getting these messages out across the profession and beyond, we are delighted to partner with the Guardian, which for many years has been the focal point of comment and opinion on fundraising and the voluntary sector. Many thanks go to Guardian Newspapers Limited for helping produce such a valuable resource to a wonderful career.

Introduction

By Patrick Butler
Editor, SocietyGuardian

Welcome to *Working in Fundraising*, a long-overdue route map to working in a sector that is rarely out of the headlines.

In the wake of a handful of charity fraud scandals, and relentlessly negative media coverage of face-to-face street fundraising, there is little doubt that fundraisers face increased scrutiny. Winning public trust and confidence has become as important as securing donations. The recent draft charities bill may have proposed self regulation for fundraising but waiting in the wings are 'reserve powers' for the home secretary to introduce statutory regulation if the sector fails in its task.

Just how successful fundraisers are in this regard is crucial. Falls in voluntary income and underperforming stock market investments are forcing many organisations to diversify their funding. This means developing new markets, techniques and fundraising talent. It is a pivotal time for the sector.

So it is encouraging to see the profession coming of age. A SocietyGuardian/Institute of Fundraising survey shows fundraising offers good opportunities for long-term career development. Graduate trainee schemes are on the increase; salaries are competitive (nearly half of fundraising directors earn £40,000 or more); professional development is growing and the sector is attracting more and more private sector 'switchers'.

And how to find work in fundraising? The best place to look for jobs is the Guardian's weekly Media Guardian supplement and the innovative Jobmatch online service. The Guardian is also proud to offer the best and most authoritative editorial coverage of fundraising and the voluntary sector, both through its weekly SocietyGuardian supplement, and every day of the week on our website, SocietyGuardian.co.uk

We wish you well in your career in fundraising.

About this guide

Working in Fundraising provides information and guidance about employment as a fundraiser. It is designed for anyone considering a career in this sector, from graduates to professionals who want to move from the private or public sectors, career returners and volunteers. For those already working in fundraising, the guide offers practical advice on professional development and career progression.

The majority of fundraisers work in the arts, charities, health, academic institutions and religious organisations. However, fundraising jobs also exist in membership associations, political parties and think tanks amongst other organisations. Wherever possible, the information in this guide covers the generic fundraising sector, with details of specialist areas and roles where available.

A unique aspect of this guide is the valuable information provided by Institute of Fundraising members about their own careers in fundraising. A total of 1,121 members responded to our joint survey conducted in February 2004 and their responses provide an excellent insight into working in fundraising.

This research is enhanced by interviews with a wide range of professional fundraisers, which form the basis for the guide's case studies. These give first-hand accounts of fundraisers' career pathways (Personal perspective) and shed light on specialist areas (Fundraising focus). The guide also draws on the Guardian's extensive coverage of fundraising and comment from a number of sector experts.

Section 1 gives an introduction to fundraising, with information on who fundraises, funding sources and key sector issues. Job opportunities are explored in Section 2, and Section 3 examines salaries and benefits. Practical advice on training, work experience and job hunting is provided in Section 4. Guidance on developing your fundraising career is contained in Section 5.

To help you research and develop your career, we have compiled a directory of over 200 fundraising resources, including recruitment consultants, training providers, events and useful publications. Many of the terms used throughout this guide will be familiar to those already working in fundraising but for newcomers to the sector, there is an extensive Glossary.

We hope that you will find *Working in Fundraising* a valuable resource and use it as a reference tool as you progress in your fundraising career. It is our intention to build on this resource in future editions so we would welcome any feedback or suggestions for additional Directory listings. You can email comments or information to working.in.fundraising@guardian.co.uk

Acknowledgements

This guide would not have been half as informative or illuminating without the contributions made by Institute of Fundraising members and other fundraisers. Their willingness to share experiences and opinions is much appreciated and adds an important facet to the guide.

A number of acknowledgements are due to other people. Many thanks to Clare Conley for researching and writing the case study interviews and additional editorial material. Thanks also to the following for their generous contributions of time and knowledge in the course of our research:

- Bill Bruty, Fundraising Training Ltd
- Lara Cely, Charity People
- Paul Farthing, Target Direct
- Janet Fleming, VSNTO
- Liz Grimes, The Kage Partnership
- Sarah Illingworth, CF Appointments
- Howard Lake, UK Fundraising
- Richard Radcliffe, Smee & Ford
- Elaine Smethurst, Working for a Charity
- Meena Varma, Directory of Social Change

I am grateful to The Kage Partnership and Remuneration Economics for supplying salary survey information, also to the Charities Aid Foundation (CAF) and the National Council for Voluntary Organisations (NCVO) for allowing us to reproduce information from their publications.

At the Institute of Fundraising, I would like to thank Fran Barlow, Lindsay Boswell, Fiona Harvey, David Parker and Andrew Watt for their guidance and valuable input throughout the project. Thanks also to Rosella Alicandro for compiling the Directory listings.

At the Guardian, a huge thank you is due to Graham Fowles and Jim Mann in the research department for their help in planning and executing the email survey.

Liza Ramrayka
September 2004

Introduction
to fundraising

Overview

What is fundraising?

'Donors don't give to institutions. They invest in ideas and people in whom they believe.'
G.T. 'Buck' Smith, US fundraiser

Fundraising is the process of generating money and other support to fund the work of an organisation, usually a charity or other not-for-profit body. Thousands of organisations in the UK simply would not survive without this support; for others, fundraising provides the means to improve, extend and innovate in their work. As such, fundraising is the lifeblood for many organisations and lies at the very heart of their operations.

And it's big business. Latest figures show that the UK's top 500 fundraising charities generated £8.6bn in 2002–03, of which more than half (£4.6bn) came from voluntary sources. There are over 12,000 professional fundraisers working in the top 500 charities while fundraising appears on the job description of thousands more paid staff working in smaller organisations. The armies of motivated and loyal volunteers who turn out to rattle tins and take part in sponsored events may be the familiar face of fundraising but behind the scenes is a professional industry staffed by highly trained individuals.

Fundraised support comes in a number of guises. These include direct donations from the public; government and lottery grants; income earned through trading activities; fees paid for contracts or services; monies generated through partnerships with the commercial sector and 'in kind' donations such as volunteer time. The common theme is that they all involve an organisation demonstrating why its work is important and why people should give money or other support.

Why do organisations need to fundraise?

Many organisations simply cannot afford to keep going without fundraising. Typically they do not make enough money each year to cover their costs. Alternatively they may need to raise funds to replace time-limited income, such as a government grant that only lasts for three years. Or fundraising may be introduced to diversify income or to avoid becoming over-dependent on income that may be subject to fluctuation (such as returns from stock market investments).

A vast number of organisations are involved in fundraising to some extent. These range from charities and schools to hospital trusts and museums. Fundraising enables them to meet their current costs, which could include:

- running existing services
- developing new projects or programmes
- maintaining buildings and vehicles
- offering grants
- paying wages

As well as covering current expenditure, fundraising can also help organisations to become financially secure in the future. One way to achieve this is to develop donors who continue to support them, through regular giving or membership fees. Another is setting up activities or events that will generate regular and lasting income. These could include trading operations or company payroll giving schemes.

Fundraising can also provide the investment capital for organisations to develop or diversify their work in response to changing demands and new markets. For example, a homelessness charity may decide to move away from providing accommodation and towards education and training for homeless people; a helpline organisation might find a lucrative market in selling counselling services to the corporate sector.

What is the fundraiser's role?
The fundraiser's job is to identify potential funders, funding opportunities and methods of generating income to meet their organisation's current or future spending plans. Fundraising is all about building relationships; a fundraiser's job is not only to attract the donor but to cultivate a relationship with them so that they continue to give, maintain an interest in the organisation or get involved in its work.

According to the Institute of Fundraising's code of conduct for members, fundraisers should demonstrate competence in:

- establishing and communicating a case for support
- planning, organising and monitoring the allocation of resources
- research, analysis and strategy development
- coping with change and problem solving
- ability to work with colleagues, suppliers and others to achieve fundraising objectives.

Fundraising organisations often use external specialists to raise money on their behalf. These organisations include specialists in face-to-face fundraising, telephone fundraising, direct marketing agencies, database companies and prospect researchers. Who's Who in Fundraising (published by the Institute of Fundraising) includes a directory of fundraising consultancies.

Changing market conditions and the influence of government policies are among the factors that can affect the fundraiser's role. And competition can be tough: charities, schools, hospitals and universities are among the many fundraising organisations jostling for public donations, corporate support and statutory grants. The role of the fundraiser is to use their skills, experience and the means at their disposal to make the 'ask' using the most appropriate method for their target market.

❶ *See* **Section 2** *for more about jobs in fundraising and* **Section 3** *for information about salaries and benefits*

❶ *See* **Sections 4** *and* **5** *for information about finding a job in fundraising and career progression*

❶ *See* **Glossary** *for an explanation of common fundraising terms*

Who fundraises?

There are thousands of organisations in the UK who rely on fundraising to operate. The majority of these are 'not-for-profit' organisations, which are involved in work of benefit to the public and do not make a profit, or reinvest revenue in order to achieve their social objectives.

According to the UK Voluntary Sector Almanac 2004, the sector (which includes charities, voluntary organisations, community groups and non-profit bodies such as universities) had a total income of £20.8bn in 2001–02. Charity Trends, published annually by the Charities Aid Foundation (CAF), lists the top 500 fundraising charities and the top 500 grantmakers.

❶ *See* **Directory** *for more information about the UK Voluntary Sector Almanac and Charity Trends*

Fundraising organisations include:

Arts organisations
Fundraising helps organisations that are involved in creating or hosting arts activities to supplement income from ticket or entrance fees. These organisations include art galleries, arts venues, ballet and other dance groups, museums, opera companies, orchestras and theatres.

The biggest source of arts funding are the national and regional arts councils of England, Scotland, Wales and Northern Ireland, who distribute public money from government and the national lottery. Local authorities are the second largest supporter of arts organisations, providing funding for organisations and events. However council funding of the arts is discretionary so they are not required to do so.

Arts organisations also raise funds through company sponsorship and applying for grants from trusts and foundations. Some organisations are heavily dependent on fundraising for income. Museums and galleries for example generated £68m through fundraising in 2002-03, compared to just £22m from trading.

Individuals give around £236m to the arts each year, over half of which (52%) goes to heritage and around three-quarters (73%) to London-based organisations.

The Department for Culture, Media and Sport (www.culture.gov.uk) provides information about funding for the arts through the national and regional arts councils.

The top five arts institutions and museums by voluntary income (£m) in 2001–02 were:

1. English National Opera (28.5)
2. Royal Opera House, Covent Garden Ltd (26.4)
3. Victoria and Albert Museum (23.2)
4. Tate (18.8)
5. Royal Shakespeare Theatre, Stratford upon Avon (16.2)
   Source: Charity Trends 2004

Charities and voluntary organisations

Charities, voluntary organisations and community groups are organisations that are set up with the objective of addressing a social need, rather than merely to generate revenue. As such, they usually rely on fundraising to support their activities.

These organisations – sometimes referred to collectively as the voluntary and community sector – range from small community groups to large, national charities with local branches. Their work supports areas such as children, crime, disability, the environment, medical research, older people and social welfare. Their activities include providing services or facilities; advice and information; work and grantmaking. This sector also includes campaign groups involved in work to change government policies or public attitudes and housing associations.

There are over 188,730 registered charities in the UK, the majority of which have an income of £10,000 or less – or around 1% of the total income of all registered charities. Just over 7% of charities receive nearly 90% of the total annual income recorded; the largest 471 charities attract over 45% of total income.

The Charity Commission (www.charity-commission.gov.uk) maintains an online listing of registered charities. CAF (www.cafonline.org) provides information for the public and charities about charitable

Fundraising focus: arts fundraising

Angela McCloskey has the challenge of raising £12m over the next three years. As development manager – capital campaign, at the Lyric Theatre in Belfast, her job involves running a capital appeal to rebuild the theatre and fund a studio – vital for developing new work and educational projects given that the Lyric is the only 'producing' venue left in Northern Ireland giving local writers and actors (including Liam Neeson, now a patron) the chance to develop.

According to McCloskey, a lottery application was the first step for the capital appeal. This demanded detailed architecture designs and a five-year business plan. Bids to trusts and foundations, the local authority and the government via the Department of Culture, Arts and Leisure are also part of McCloskey's fundraising strategy. The appeal will also include organising public fundraising events and corporate sponsorship.

Day-to-day fundraising is split between different roles. Education and outreach staff source funds for their projects while the marketing manager handles corporate sponsorship. McCloskey says competition can be tough in arts fundraising: there is heavy demand for lottery funding while local councils have different agendas, prioritising some arts above others for funding. Fundraisers may also have to compete against very emotive charitable causes for public donations.

So tapping into the creativity of the people working in the arts is an important fundraising ploy, she says. For instance, the theatre's artistic director plays a vital role in communicating to potential funders the excitement and importance of what the theatre does.

giving. The Voluntary Agencies Directory (published annually by NCVO, www.ncvo-vol.org.uk) lists over 2,000 voluntary organisations active in the UK.

The top 10 fundraising sectors by voluntary income (£m) in 2002–3 were:

1. International (654)
2. Cancer (417)
3. Religious – general services (356)
4. Heritage/environment (351)
5. Arts/culture (341)
6. Children (321)
7. Religious missionary (290)
8. Animal protection/rescue (257)
9. General social welfare (241)
10. Disability (181)

Source: Charity Trends 2004

Top 20 fundraising charities by voluntary income, 2002–03

Charity	Voluntary income (£m)
Cancer Research UK	243.541
National Trust	160.583
Oxfam	131.126
British Heart Foundation	112.015
Royal National Lifeboat Institution (RNLI)	95.600
Salvation Army	90.064
NSPCC	79.459
Comic Relief	73.735
Macmillan Cancer Relief	71.070
RSPCA	68.159
British Red Cross Society	64.591
Marie Curie Cancer Care	63.591
Save the Children UK	62.891
Help the Aged	59.896
PDSA	57.937
RSPB	53.219
Barnardo's	50.810
RNIB	49.894
ActionAid	47.926
Church of Scotland Unincorporated Boards	45.701

Source: Charity Trends 2004

Healthcare

Hospitals, hospices and other healthcare providers receive a large proportion of their funding from the NHS but many also rely on fundraising to support their work.

A hospital trust (or NHS trust) will fundraise to provide additional support and services to those it runs within the community. These could include a new hospital wing or a library. If it is a regional or national centre of expertise, it may need to raise funds to provide specialist care or medical equipment.

The most common sources of this income include legacies; community fundraising with schools, local organisations and individuals; corporate fundraising through partnerships with local, regional and national business, and donations or grants from charitable trusts and foundations. A hospital trust or hospice might organise its fundraising through a separate charity or through a 'friends of' voluntary organisation.

The NHS website (www.nhs.uk) contains information about the role of hospital trusts and a searchable database of all UK hospitals. The Department of Health (www.dh.gov.uk) provides information about hospital and hospice funding.

The top five fundraising hospitals and hospices by voluntary income (£m) in 2002–03 were:

1. The Benenden Hospital Trust (19.7)
2. Great Ormond Street Hospital Children's Charity (18.9)
3. Christie Hospital Charitable Fund (16.6)
4. The Royal Marsden Hospital Charity (8.8)
5. University College London Hospitals Charities (7.1)

Source: Charity Trends 2004

Fundraising focus: NHS fundraising

The perception that all aspects of the NHS are paid for by direct taxation is one of the key challenges that NHS fundraisers have to overcome. In fact, hospitals were funded by charity before the NHS was set up in 1948 and charitable giving has continued to help buy equipment, pay for specialist staff and improve buildings since its inception.

Dealing with the complexities of large organisations is another challenge for NHS fundraisers, according to Charlotte Langley, the joint director of fundraising for both the London-based Guy's and St Thomas' NHS Trust (one of the largest NHS trusts in the country) and its charitable foundation.

Langley reports to two line managers from the trust and the foundation, and manages joint appeals. She directs a multi-skilled fundraising team of four, working to reach a fundraising target of £10m for the Evelina Appeal, currently her main focus. This is needed to build a seven-storey children's hospital on the St Thomas' site.

The foundation awards grants for a range of new services, research and development: £300,000 has been granted for a project to encourage local young people to use sexual health services, for example. More money is needed to fund the art collection, which aims to improve the hospital environment, and schemes to encourage patients' creativity to aid their recovery.

Networking with wealthy individuals is a vital part of securing the necessary funds – one has pledged a gift of £1 m. This area of fundraising requires research, cultivation, preparation combined with personal presentations and site visits, according to Langley.

She has also secured HRH the Princess Royal as a patron for the Evelina Appeal, which is a boost for major gift fundraising. But fundraising by the local communities of Lambeth and Southwark is equally important, says Langley. Rotary clubs, scout groups and schools are just some of the groups that get involved and make valuable contributions.

Membership associations

The top 10 professional associations receive a total of £17m each year in voluntary support. Many of these interest-based organisations are related to medical professions and include the Royal College of Surgeons, Royal College of General Practitioners and Royal College of Nursing.

Political parties

Political parties rely heavily on donations to fund their campaign work between and around election time. These donations come from individual supporters, companies and trade unions. Parties use membership and supporter schemes to raise funds from individual supporters. Falling membership numbers have seen the rise of 'affinity' deals, where members receive discounts with partner organisations such as insurers or utility companies. Party fundraisers also develop links with business to encourage large donations and organise commercial events to target key donors such as wealthy individuals.

The Electoral Commission (www.electoralcommission.gov.uk) publishes information about donations to political parties. The Guardian's politics website (www.guardian.co.uk/politics) includes coverage of party funding.

Religious organisations

Churches, mosques, temples and other places of worship rely on fundraising to help them to maintain buildings and to offer services to the local community. Faith-based charities raised £350m in voluntary income in 2002–3. Most organisations enlist the help of volunteers to organise fundraising activities but a professional fundraiser may be employed to run a large project, such as a major appeal for building repairs, or to head an appeal committee. As well as working with individual donors, religious organisations might also approach local companies for sponsorship. Other funding sources include local authorities, grantmaking trusts and government grants through agencies such as the Heritage Lottery Fund.

Schools and colleges

Educational establishments such as schools and colleges have a long tradition of fundraising, through the involvement of parents and pupils in activities. Many schools still rely on voluntary fundraising through PTAs (parent teacher associations) to raise money for books, sports equipment, buildings and extracurricular activities. However, an increasing number of schools and colleges, particularly those in the independent sector, now include fundraising in the brief of a paid member of staff (e.g. bursar, business manager), or employ a specialist to coordinate fundraising activity. Often this shifts the focus from organising one-off fundraising events to encouraging regular giving by parents and ex-students, legacy donations or major gifts from business.

Ofsted, the office for standards in education (www.ofsted.gov.uk) maintains a searchable database of all UK schools and publishes inspection reports on state and independent schools.

Sports organisations

Fundraising and sponsorship is big business not only for high profile football clubs and motor racing teams but also for thousands of local sports groups. Government and lottery funding are significant sources of support for these organisations, which rely on fundraising to pay for equipment, to improve or build facilities and to cover travel costs.

The money raised for sport by the National Lottery is shared by five distributing bodies: Sport England, the Sports Council for Wales, Sportscotland, Sports Council for Northern Ireland and UK Sport. Other funders include sports charity, the Football Foundation and the government-backed Sportsmatch scheme which matches business sponsorship gained by grassroots clubs. UK Sport maintains a searchable database of the national sports councils, sports governing bodies and partner organisations that it works with, which is accessible via its website (www.uksport.gov.uk)

Think tanks

Independent think tanks – organisations that produce ideas and knowledge for discussion in the public arena and on the political stage – depend on fundraising to fund their research and information work. The top voluntary income earners include the New Economics Foundation, Institute for Public Policy Research and Forum for the Future. The Guardian's politics website (www.guardian.co.uk/politics) includes a listing of the main think tanks in the UK and details of their area of work.

Universities

As government funding for UK universities becomes increasingly tight, many institutions now count on fundraising to plug the gaps left by insufficient grant and fee income. The top 10 universities account for almost a quarter (24%) of this income, with £3.5bn between them (Source: Charity Trends 2003)

The UK universities with the highest income (£m) in 2002–03 were:

1. The University of Cambridge   464.834
2. The University of Oxford   457.932
3. University College London   457.929
4. Imperial College of Science, Technology & Medicine   409.304
5. University of Manchester   362.968

Source: HESA Resources of Higher Education Institutions 2002/03

[HESA - Higher Education Statistics Agency]

Universities fundraise to meet the costs of scholarships and hardship funds; establish new teaching and research posts; replace outdated equipment or buildings and create new amenities.

A university might employ a fundraiser in its public affairs team, marketing department or, increasingly, in a dedicated 'development' office. Potential donors include alumni, local business and grantmaking trusts. Income generation methods include supporter schemes and high profile fundraising events.

In the US, university endowment funds are more well established than in the UK due to a culture of voluntary giving being encouraged there during the 1970s and 1980s. Harvard now boasts an endowment fund of $18bn a year, compared to Oxford University's £2bn fund. A UK government task force report in 2004 concluded that universities could generate up to £600m a year by investing in setting up dedicated fundraising offices. Universities UK (www.universitiesuk.ac.uk) is the membership body that represents all UK universities and some colleges of higher education.

Regulators and professional bodies

Charity Commission (www.charity-commission.gov.uk)

The Charity Commission is established by law as the regulator and registrar for charities in England and Wales. Its activities include checking that charities are run for public benefit, and not for private advantage; ensuring that charities are independent, and detecting and remedying serious mismanagement or deliberate abuse by or within charities. In Scotland, this role is carried out by the Office of the Scottish Charity Regulator (www.oscr.org.uk), which is an agency of the Scottish Executive.

Home Office (www.homeoffice.gov.uk)

The Home Office is the government department with responsibility for regulating public collections for charities. It approves local authority regulations governing collections which are made in the street. It also makes orders which exempt charities from the need to apply to a local authority for permission to do a collection house to house. Where a local authority refuses a licence for a house-to-house collection the Home Office will consider any appeal which the charity may lodge against the local authority's refusal.

Inland Revenue (www.inlandrevenue.gov.uk)

Inland Revenue administers the repayment to charities of taxes from which they are exempt (e.g. income tax, corporation tax), including tax claims in respect of Gift Aid donations. It also produces tax guidance for charities on a range of issues, including fundraising events (in conjunction with HM Customs & Excise).

HM Customs & Excise (www.hmce.gov.uk)

HM Customers & Excise provides guidance to charities on VAT registration and VAT exemption in areas such as fundraising events.

Institute of Fundraising (www.institute-of-fundraising.org.uk)

The Institute of Fundraising represents fundraisers and fundraising throughout the UK. It is a membership organisation, with 4,000 individual members and nearly 200 organisational members who agree to abide by its code of conduct. The Institute promotes best practice through its codes of fundraising practice, which cover different areas of fundraising activity. It has also produced a donor's charter, which sets out a fundraiser's commitment to donors and a complaints procedure.

ⓘ *See* **About the Institute** *section for more on the code of conduct and codes of fundraising practice*

The Professional Fundraising Regulatory Association (www.pfra.org.uk)

The PFRA is a voluntary self-regulatory body for organisations involved in fundraising by direct debit on the street and door to door. Its membership includes over 100 charities and professional fundraising companies. Members abide by the Institute of Fundraising codes of practice and face checks from the organisation's 'mystery shoppers'. The PFRA has also set up an accreditation scheme for street fundraisers.

ⓘ *See* **Directory** *section for full contact details of organisations above*

Also see Directory for other relevant professional bodies such as the Chartered Institute of Marketing, Direct Marketing Association and Institute of Direct Marketing.

Sector snapshot: Regulation in fundraising

In 2002, a major review of charity law and regulation concluded that there should be a new self-regulatory initiative to promote good practice in fundraising. The review, conducted by the Strategy Unit of the Cabinet Office, recommended a new independent body to oversee this initiative. It also called for a simplified licensing system for public collections to be introduced.

The government's draft charities bill published in May 2004 backed these ideas by proposing self-regulation, rather than state regulation, for fundraisers. The draft bill says that government expects self-regulation to ensure that all fundraisers refrain from making 'unreasonably persistent approaches' or applying 'undue pressure' when fundraising. Under the proposals, the home secretary would have reserve powers to introduce statutory regulation if self-regulation is not sufficiently robust.

Fundraisers and their regulators are currently debating what form self regulation will take. Ideas include an independent complaints body – the Charity Fundraising Standards Board – for members of the public. The board would include representatives from other consumer-focused bodies, observers from government regulators such as the Charity Commission and a representative from the membership body that regulated fundraising organisations must join.

The draft bill also proposes a simplified licensing system for public collections, to be administered by local authorities. This will bring direct debit collections – such as face-to-face fundraising – into licensing arrangements alongside street and door-to-door collections. A group bringing together charities, police, local authorities, umbrella groups and the Charity Commission will take forward work on the practical details of the scheme. The anticipated bill will affect all registered charities in England and Wales if implemented.

To read the draft charities bill, visit www.homeoffice.gov.uk/comrace/active/charitylaw/index.html

Where does the money come from?

Fundraising organisations derive their income and other support from a wide range of sources. The main ones are:

- the general public
- the public sector (e.g. UK government, European Union)
- the private sector (e.g. corporate sponsors)
- the voluntary sector (e.g. grantmaking trusts)
- internal sources (e.g. income from trading)

Latest figures from NCVO show that the public sector is becoming a more important source of income for charities and voluntary organisations. There is also a shift away from voluntary income (income given freely as a donation or grant) towards earned income (income from sales of goods and services). However, voluntary income still accounts for almost half the voluntary sector's income and was worth £9.8bn in 2001–02.

Income types and sources

Source of income	TYPE OF INCOME Earned income	Voluntary income	Investment returns
Individuals	Fees for services provided (e.g. residential home fees, tickets to events) Fees for goods (e.g. catalogue sales) Membership subscriptions with significant benefits	Individual donations (gross, including Gift Aid reclaimed) Covenants Legacies Membership subscriptions without significant benefits	
Public sector	Public sector fees and payments for contracted services	Project grants Core funding grants Grants to charitable intermediaries Grants from National Lottery distributors	
Private sector	Sponsorship Research or consultancy services Patent royalties	Corporate grants and gifts	
Voluntary sector	Services provided under contract (e.g. membership fees)	Grants from charitable trusts	
Internal sources	Gross turnover of trading subsidiaries	Grants distributed by charitable intermediaries	Dividends Interest payments on securities Rent from investment property Bank and building society interest

Source: The UK Voluntary Sector Almanac 2004

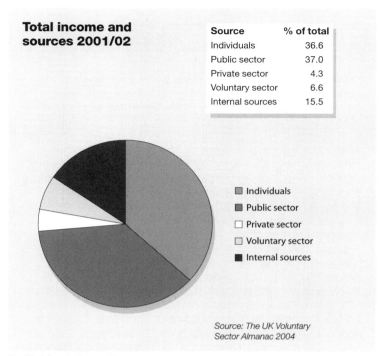

Total income and sources 2001/02

Source	% of total
Individuals	36.6
Public sector	37.0
Private sector	4.3
Voluntary sector	6.6
Internal sources	15.5

- Individuals
- Public sector
- Private sector
- Voluntary sector
- Internal sources

Source: The UK Voluntary Sector Almanac 2004

Individual donations

The UK public gives £7bn to good causes each year. Individuals contribute to street and door-to-door collections (still the most popular methods of giving) and through one-off activities such as buying a charity raffle ticket or attending a fundraising event. They can also take part in payroll giving or donate shares to charity. Direct mail campaigns, telemarketing, internet fundraising and direct response TV campaigns are among the methods used by organisations to get individual donors to pledge donations.

Organisations also use fundraising appeals to attract donations from individuals. An appeal might seek to raise funds for a particular group of beneficiaries, such as older or homeless people. Or it might aim to raise capital to develop facilities and equipment, needed by organisations such as hospitals and schools. Individuals who make large donations (also known as big gifts) are called major donors.

Legacies

Legacies are one of the most important sources of charitable income, representing around £1.5bn each year. There are several types of legacy but all involve an individual specifying in their will that they wish to leave money or other assets to charity.

Sector spotlight: Legacy fundraising

By Richard Radcliffe, chairman – Smee & Ford, legacy fundraising consultancy

The last decade has proved that anyone wanting to be a legacy fundraiser is not heading into a dead end job. This period has seen a minor revolution in terms of legacy income performance and investment in legacy fundraising.

The service provision of local community organisations is often more tangible locally than big national charities so the need for legacies can easily be communicated locally. Smaller charities find it easier to meet limited numbers of stakeholders – building trust and confidence through personal contact is perfect legacy fundraising. You can integrate legacies into all activities at little, or even no, cost so there is no risk – but with the average legacy valued at around £16,000 the effect on local organisations can be life saving.

Legacy fundraisers need common sense and good communication skills above all else. As long as you are good with people, sensitive to family environments, have a broad understanding of why people support charities and can write and talk clearly, then the legacy world is your oyster.

Many charities are now merging legacy fundraising either into major gift departments or into donor development. The sense of isolation of legacy fundraisers, which was so prevalent 10 years ago, has largely disappeared. It is possible to remain in legacy fundraising for many years, meeting challenges every day and developing new skills. And if you want to aim for major gift management, senior strategic positions, or donor development then the routes are now open.

The top five fundraising charities by legacy income (£m) in 2002–03 were:

1. Cancer Research UK (113.6)
2. Royal National Lifeboat Institution (RNLI) (68.5)
3. National Trust (45.1)
4. RSPCA (43.8)
5. British Heart Foundation (38.3)

Source: Charity Trends 2004

Many organisations are heavily reliant on legacies. At RNLI for example, six out of every 10 lifeboat launches are funded by legacy gifts. For other organisations, legacies are part of the fundraising mix.

Research by MORI in 2003 shows that the number of people who had recently made a will including a legacy was around 8%. The sector-led Legacy Promotion Campaign aims to increase this figure by 2% by 2006, to generate an extra £180m for charities. LPC's Remember A

Personal perspective: Will Coffin

Job: Individual donor and legacy fundraising manager

Organisation: CSV (Community Service Volunteers)

Age: 33

Legacy fundraising inevitably involves getting people to think about death and that's a difficult subject to broach. We use a network of advocates or champions at CSV – usually older volunteers who have already pledged a legacy and will tell others of the benefits.

Targets for legacy fundraising are based on pledges and if a 60-year-old makes a legacy, the charity may not receive the money for 20 years or more. It's also difficult to persuade people to tell you how much they are planning to give and all of these factors can make this area of fundraising unpredictable and quite difficult to evaluate.

CSV carried out its first legacy campaign last year, before I joined. I plan to develop a new direct marketing strategy to build on this. I work three days a week here as part of a fundraising team of five. We need to raise more than £2m a year to continue helping a million people a year to change their lives for the better by volunteering.

Prior to joining CSV I spent seven years in various fundraising and media roles at Christian Aid before leaving to take an MA in political behaviour. And once the fundraising strategy is in place at CSV, in a few years time I'd like to emigrate to Mexico, learn Spanish and set up a B&B.

Charity campaign (www.rememberacharity.org.uk) involves around 120 charities working together to promote legacy donations through the consumer and legal press and direct mail.

Committed giving

Getting donors to give on a regular basis is an important part of an organisation's fundraising. This committed or regular giving provides a continuing income stream and helps organisations to plan their work. Regular donations also enable charities to claim back tax if they are made tax-effectively.

Fundraisers recruit these donors using techniques such as direct mail campaigns, door-to-door fundraising and face-to-face street fundraising (see below). Methods of committed giving include:

- regular donations – often made monthly, collected by direct debit and tax efficient if the donor uses the Gift Aid scheme
- payroll giving – regular, usually monthly payments from an employee's wages
- membership schemes – monthly or annual fees paid in return for special benefits or opportunities to participate in an organisation's work.

Getting Britain Giving

Getting Britain Giving is the name of a UK government campaign to implement the measures announced in the 2000 Budget to make charitable giving more tax effective. The package of measures included abolition of the £250 minimum limit for Gift Aid donations (which attract an extra 28p from the Treasury for every £1 given); removal of the £1,200 a year ceiling for payroll giving and the introduction of a 10% government supplement on all payroll donations for three years, subsequently extended until 2004.

The Giving Campaign

The Giving Campaign was launched in July 2001 as a national three-year initiative to encourage a culture of giving and to increase the amount of money given to UK charities. Backed by government and the voluntary sector, the campaign focused on four areas: targeting wealthy people, tax-effective giving, employers and employees, and young people.

Activities included the launch of a new brand for Gift Aid (now used by 60% of charities); promotion of payroll giving; involvement of financial advisors in encouraging individual donations and a schools-based programme – Giving Nation – to promote charity to young people. Individual giving has risen by more than £0.5bn to £7bn a year during the lifetime of the campaign.

ⓘ▸ *The Inland Revenue (www.inlandrevenue.gov.uk) has further information about Gift Aid and payroll giving*

ⓘ▸ *Further information about the Giving Campaign and tax-effective giving is at www.givingcampaign.org.uk*

ⓘ▸ *For more about Giving Nation, visit www.g-nation.co.uk*

Research by the Centre for Interfirm Comparison shows that committed giving increased by 18% in 2003 and has increased by 70% over the past three years. It now accounts for 17% of charities' voluntary income and is the second biggest voluntary income source after legacies.

Face-to-face fundraising

Face-to-face or direct dialogue fundraising involves fundraisers approaching people in the street or other public places to encourage them to sign up to a direct debit to support an organisation. The fundraiser might work for a professional fundraising organisation (PFO) employed by the organisation, or be part of the organisation's in-house team.

Introduced from Austria by the environmental charity Greenpeace in 1997, face-to-face fundraising was responsible for recruiting 690,000 new, committed supporters in 2002, whose pledges are worth £240m to the voluntary sector over the next five years. Organisations such as Amnesty International have found that this method helps them to recruit donors from a younger age group.

The organisation usually pays a flat rate fee per donor to the fundraising firm. The longer the donor maintains the direct debit, the greater the return to the organisation on its investment. Donations are eligible for Gift Aid.

Fundraisers are expected to comply with good practice recommended by the Institute of Fundraising and the Professional Fundraising Regulatory Association. The spread of face-to-face has made the fundraisers difficult to avoid in major cities, earning them the nickname 'chuggers' (charity muggers).

Payroll giving

Payroll giving is an increasingly popular tax effective way of donating to charity. It enables employees to make donations direct from their gross salary, so if a basic rate taxpayer wants to give a £10 donation, it will only cost £7.80, or £6 for higher-rate taxpayers. This method generated £86m for charities in 2002-03, during which time around 1,000 companies launched schemes for their employees.

The rise in payroll giving to good causes from £55m in 2000-01 is due largely to a government scheme that saw the Treasury adding 10% to every donation until April 2004 (see Getting Britain Giving, above). Payroll giving is a very easy form of giving from a donor's perspective. For the recipient organisation, it offers a regular and reliable source of income that allows them to plan ahead. Employees who donate may also be interested in fundraising or volunteering for the organisation.

Many companies promote a scheme as part of their corporate social responsibility programme to boost employee morale, or to complement existing volunteering or charity 'adoption' schemes. Some employers match their employees' payroll donations, which can sometimes double the income to an organisation.

Charities often use a professional fundraising organisation (PFO) to promote these donations in the workplace, with payments processed through a separate payroll giving agency. The largest payroll giving scheme is Give As Your Earn, administered by the Charities Aid Foundation (www.allaboutgiving.org).

ⓘ *The Inland Revenue (www.inlandrevenue.gov.uk) has further information about payroll giving, PFOs and agencies*

Payroll giving helped Save the Children to raise £958,703 in 2002-03. Company matching donations and post-tax giving took the charity's overall figure for payroll donations to £1.4 m. Of considerable impact was a matching arrangement with the Royal Bank of Scotland Group, which doubles individual staff donations up to £100. As a result, RBS and its employees contributed £59,393 to the charity in 2002–03.

Membership schemes

Membership schemes offer organisations another method of securing regular, long-term support from donors. Typically they involve an individual paying a monthly or annual fee to become a member of the organisation. In return the organisation might offer discounted entry to a venue (as National Trust members receive) or exclusive benefits (such as the Tate Modern's members-only room). Alternatively members might be invited to campaign or express support for the organisation's work, as in the case of Friends of the Earth.

Events and challenges

Fundraising events are a tried and tested method of raising money, involving volunteers and attracting new donors. Traditional activities include flag days and fetes. Music concerts, charity auctions and festivals are other examples. Events income can come from selling tickets and securing corporate sponsorship.

Organisations can also raise funds through sponsored walks and runs, where individuals secure sponsorship from friends and family to participate in an activity. Challenge events have become a popular form of charity fundraising. Typically these involve individuals or teams (often company employees) raising sponsorship to take part in an activity such as an overseas bike ride or UK mountain climb. Participants must usually reach a minimum sponsorship level in order to take part. The events are often organised for the charity by an external company. Many companies use charity challenges as morale and team building exercises for their employees.

Appeals

Charities and other organisations often use fundraising appeals to raise a large sum of money in a short space of time. These might target their members, supporters, the general public or all three. Many are supported by fundraising events (e.g BBC Children in Need, Live Aid) or are linked with awareness raising (e.g. the Royal British Legion's poppy appeal).

Overseas relief and development agencies often use appeals to raise money for disasters. Heritage or environmental organisations might launch a public appeal to fund the preservation of an historic property or species of wildlife. The National Trust's 2002 appeal to save the

Fundraising focus: Celebrity fundraising

Reading the popular press – tabloids and magazines like Hello!, OK!, Heat, Now as well as the Stage, the Radio Times and the TV Times – isn't just a leisure-time pursuit for celebrity fundraisers; it's a vital part of their job. Constant research into popular culture and current affairs enables them to match the right celebrity with the right event or appeal.

Children's charity NCH does not seek to fundraise directly from celebrities as major donors, although some charities do. It aims to develop relationships whereby celebrities lend their high profile to boost fundraising and awareness-raising activities. Richard White, celebrity supporter manager at the charity, manages a team of four, working mainly with fundraisers and the press office across the organisation to source around 300 celebrities a year for over 200 events. These range from film premiers and black-tie dinners to angling competitions and sponsored walks.

Risk management and planning are key to working with celebrities, who may pull out at the last minute due to changes in filming schedules. Liaising with agents and building relationships with celebrities, based on trust, are also important aspects of the job. Managing staff expectations within the charity presents another challenge, as everyone wants an 'A list' celebrity at their event, even if it is a summer fete in Skegness on a rainy bank holiday!

Victorian estate of Tyntesfield near Bristol raised over £1.5m in 50 days from over 50,000 donations across the world.

Press advertising, telethons and online appeals are among the methods used to raise funds in this area.

Community fundraising

Raising money from local communities is another lucrative income stream for fundraisers. A national organisation might work with local supporters, volunteers and business to form a local group that will organise fundraising events. Or it might build relationships with existing community groups, such as churches and other religious bodies, sports clubs and trade unions. These groups can encourage their members or participants to fundraise or volunteer for the organisation.

Fundraising in schools represents another valuable income source. It is estimated that schools raise around £35m for charity each year. Of this £15m comes from state primary schools; £14m by state secondary schools while independent secondary schools are largely responsible for the remainder. As well as helping schools to organise fundraising events, organisations can work with students to devise teaching materials (often

linked to citizenship classes as part of the national curriculum) or
involve them in volunteering.

Retail and trading

Funds raised from selling goods and services provide many organisations
with a large part of their income. The UK Voluntary Sector Almanac 2003
estimates that the voluntary sector earned £8.9bn of its total income from
these areas in 2001-02. Charity shops are the familiar face of retail
operations, selling donated and new goods such as clothes and books;
museums, art galleries and heritage organisations often have a visitor
shop. Many organisations also sell goods (e.g. Christmas cards, products
made by charity beneficiaries or gift items) through mail order catalogues,
via their website and through partner organisations.

Charities often generate income through separate trading subsidiaries
controlled by the parent charity. Examples include the Salvation Army's
textile recycling business, which contributed to the charity's overall
trading income of £23m in 2002. Help the Aged's home shopping and

Sector snapshot: Internet fundraising
by Howard Lake, publisher – UK Fundraising

The first appeals on the web in the UK occurred at the end of 1994 and
into 1995 (Friends of the Earth and an appeal in aid of the Shakespeare
Globe Theatre), although it was not until 1998–99 that the larger UK
charities started addressing online fundraising in any noticeable way.

It is estimated that somewhere between 0.5% and 1% of total
voluntary income is received online. Websites and e-mail campaigns
do, of course, generate other additional income that is received offline,
for instance by post or via the telephone.

Often donors choose to give online in preference to the telephone,
especially in response to emergency appeals. Comic Relief has led the
way in terms of the largest amount of money raised online in a short
time: in March 2001 it raised £1.75m in seven hours, which rose
to £3.6m after two weeks (including the Gift Aid tax reclaim).
Two years previously, it had raised £330,000 online in seven hours.
Macmillan Cancer Relief raised over £250,000 in 2003 from event
sign-ups via the web, with an additional £70,000-plus from merchandise
sold online.

Some charities have recruited specifically for an online fundraiser
or new media fundraiser, but they tend to be the larger ones such as
Oxfam. In most other organisations, the online fundraising role will
usually be handled by the direct marketing fundraiser. Alternatively,
each fundraiser will be encouraged to use the web to promote their
own activities.

financial services division offers insurance and funeral planning services. Selling services to the statutory and commercial sectors is another income stream.

Central and local government

Over one third of the voluntary sector's annual £20bn income now comes from statutory sources. Income from government agencies (including overseas agencies) accounts for 37% of total income – some £7.7bn. Most of this is received by large national charities for delivering services in areas such as care, health, and education and training. By contrast, small local charities receive on average just 11% of their income from government and 50% from the public.

Government grants are designed to meet the policy objectives and programme outcomes of the awarding department. The main central government funders include the Home Office, the Department for Education and Skills, the Department for International Development, the Department of Health and the Government Offices of the Regions. Departments sometimes work together to offer grants jointly through special funds or programmes. These include Connexions, the Children's Fund and the New Deal for Disabled People.

Funding is also available from non-departmental public bodies (NDPBs) which are usually national bodies that operate at arm's length from central government. They include the national arts and sports councils, Housing Corporation and Countryside Agency.

Local and regional government are responsible for many grants aimed at supporting local and community initiatives. Smaller grants schemes are also administered for government by voluntary organisations and community foundations.

ⓘ *The governmentfunding.org.uk website offers information about grants from four central government departments: the Home Office, the Department of Health, the Department for Education and Skills and the Office of the Deputy Prime Minister*

ⓘ *A list of all government departments and local authorities can be found at www.direct.gov.uk*

Europe

The European Union provides funding for social and economic development in its member states. Most of the funding available to voluntary organisations comes from the European Regional Development Fund (ERDF) and the European Social Fund (ESF) and is administered by the Government Offices for the Regions.

ⓘ *The governmentfunding.org.uk website has information about fundraising from Europe*

National Lottery

The National Lottery is the largest source of funding for voluntary organisations, channelling £550m into charities in 2001-02. Medium-sized organisations – those with an annual income of between £100,000 and £1m – are the biggest recipients of lottery funding, which accounts for 5% of their income. The largest general charities receive less than 1% of their income from lottery funds.

Established by Parliament in 1994, the National Lottery is the responsibility of the Department for Media, Culture and Sport but run under licence by Camelot, a private sector consortium. Good causes are allocated 28p out of every £1 generated from weekly lottery games and scratchcard sales.

From 2004, a new distributor will control around half the good causes money raised by the National Lottery. The Big Lottery Fund will distribute grants previously distributed by the Community Fund and New Opportunities Fund. It will continue to fund charities and the voluntary sector, health, education and the environment, but will also take on the Millennium Commission's remit of funding large-scale regeneration projects.

Lottery funds are also distributed by the Heritage Lottery Fund and the national arts and sports councils. Grant schemes include Awards for All, which draws funds from all five sources to make grants to small organisations with an annual income of less than £15,000.

ⓘ *Links to all the lottery distributing bodies websites can be found at www.lotterygoodcauses.org.uk*

ⓘ *Information about the Awards for All is at www.awardsforall.org.uk*

Companies

Corporate giving involves a company supporting an organisation through financial and 'in kind' donations. It might do this by making a straightforward cash gift to its chosen organisation or sponsoring an event or project. Alternatively it might donate equipment, products or company facilities. Or the support might be through cause-related marketing (CRM), where a company links with a charity or other organisation to promote a product or service for mutual benefit.

Companies often involve employees in their giving activities, through staff fundraising and payroll giving schemes. Employees might also volunteer their expertise or time to help an organisation. Corporate giving accounts for a relatively small percentage of voluntary sector income. In 2001-02, the figure stood at 4.3%, compared to around 36% from the general public.

The top five corporate donors by worldwide community involvement in 2002–03 were:

1. GlaxoSmithKline plc
2. BP plc
3. Barclays plc
4. Lloyds TSB Group plc
5. BT Group

Aside from purely philanthropic reasons, companies might support an organisation because it is related to its business (e.g. environmental charity and mining company) or will help it to reach potential customers. It is increasingly common for companies to build in corporate giving to their corporate responsibility strategies.

ⓘ▸ *Business in the Community (www.bitc.org.uk) provides information about cause related marketing and other forms of company giving*

Grantmaking trusts and foundations

Grantmaking trusts – also known as foundations – are independent grantmaking bodies. Each year they distribute around £2bn to charities (including universities and religious organisations) and voluntary organisations. There are around 10,000 grantmaking trusts, distributing anything from several million pounds each year to just a few thousand.

Trusts and foundations might restrict their grants to a particular beneficiary group (e.g. BME groups or children) or field (e.g. arts or environment). The most common areas funded are arts, health, social welfare and recreation. Examples of trusts include large academic, research and scientific trusts such as the Wellcome Trust and Wolfson Foundation; grantmaking charities such as British Heart Foundation and Cancer Research UK; company-linked bodies such as Lloyds TSB Foundations for England and Wales and trusts that give in a particular region e.g. Bridge House Estates Trust Fund which supports London projects.

The top grantmaking charities by grants (£m) in 2002-03 were:

1. Wellcome Trust (395)
2. Community Fund (309)
3. Cancer Research UK (73.4)
4. British Heart Foundation (62.5)
5. Macmillan Cancer Relief (38.7)

Trusts tend to fund short- and medium-term initiatives or one-off schemes. They often fund projects that government or other bodies will not, such as new methods or minority groups. Trusts are usually funded through an endowment from a family, wealthy individual or company. There are over 100 registered corporate foundations in Britain, accounting for around 11% of corporate giving.

The Association of Charitable Foundations (www.acf.org.uk) promotes good practice among trusts and foundations.

Further information

The Directory at the back of this guide includes details of where to find out more about fundraising sources, techniques and latest sector developments. Resources include:

- useful organisations
- magazines and journals
- fundraising books
- websites
- events

Employment issues

Current issues

Increasing giving levels

Although individual donations to charity stand at £7bn, this represents just 0.9% of GDP, compared with 1.2% 20 years ago. In the US there is a more ingrained culture of giving with donations standing at around 15% of GDP. The Giving Campaign has suggested that individuals should consider donations in relation to affordability and aim to give around 1.5% of their annual income to charity (higher for the wealthy, lower for the less well off). To achieve this, many organisations are investing in promoting regular, planned giving (rather than ad hoc donations) and the use of tax effective methods.

Skills shortages

The voluntary sector is experiencing a shortage of fundraisers at all levels, particularly in middle management. Expansion in NHS and university fundraising has created many more opportunities but skilled staff to fill these roles are more scarce. Skills in specific areas such as trust fundraising are in particular demand.

Investment in fundraising

Many organisations are waking up to the benefits of investing in fundraising and are happy to justify these costs in terms of long-term benefit. Trustees and chief executives are realising that successful and sustainable fundraising relies on employing skilled staff and supporting them with training.

Public trust and confidence

Negative media coverage of fundraising dents public confidence in fundraisers' work. Demonstrating that fundraising is a professional sector is crucial to maintaining donations. One approach is to make fundraising information more accessible, through channels such as the GuideStar UK charity information website (www.guidestar.org.uk) which will launch in 2005.

Future issues

Charity law reform

The draft charities bill published in 2004 represents a fundamental shake-up of Britain's 400-year-old charity law. It centres on a new legal definition of charity based on providing a 'public benefit': charities will have to show they provide a public benefit in one of 12 key areas (see Charities Bill listing in Glossary). Private schools and private hospitals may retain their charitable status – and the tax breaks that go with it – but they will be under increased pressure to demonstrate how their facilities benefit the wider community.

Sector regulation

The 2004 draft charities bill proposes self-regulation for the fundraising sector. However, it also proposes reserve powers for the home secretary to intervene if self-regulation is not working. A new unified licensing system for street collections will cover face-to-face fundraising. This means local authorities will be able to restrict the number of fundraisers on the streets, depending on whether an area is getting overcrowded.

Tax-effective giving

The Giving Campaign (see above) kick-started a raft of activity around tax-efficient giving but there is still more to be done. Only 1% of UK companies currently operate a payroll giving scheme, equivalent to 2% of employees compared to 35% in the US. A government incentive for small and medium sized organisations that set up payroll giving could lead to more employers offering the scheme and more charities promoting it.

In 2002–03 UK charities reclaimed £506m from the Inland Revenue using Gift Aid, but estimates suggest that an additional £900m could be raised if all taxpaying donors used the scheme. The share giving scheme launched in the 2000 budget brought in almost £150m in 2001-02 from Britain's 12m shareholders, despite little promotion. Think tank nfpSynergy says charities could do more to promote share giving to their donors, particularly 'high value' supporters.

Government funding

Voluntary organisations now derive more of their income from the public sector than from individuals. The government is keen to see these organisations take a bigger role in public service delivery, so contracting and selling services is expected to increase.

Futurebuilders is a new government funding initiative for organisations to develop their public service delivery work or enter market to deliver particular public services. It will invest around £30,000 to several million in around 250 organisations and provide development grants of around £10,000 to others, supporting work around community cohesion, crime, education and learning, health and social care, and support for children and young people.

Major gifts and donors

Wealthy donors give around £1bn to charity each year but many fundraisers are failing to exploit this lucrative market. The number of UK millionaires is set to triple by 2010 so fundraising organisations may be investing in prospect research, legacy promotion and tax-effective giving campaigns aimed at wealthy givers.

Minority donors

Britain's ethnic minority and gay communities possess a disposable wealth of some £100bn but many fundraisers have yet to tap into this income stream. The Institute of Fundraising has set up a special interest group to promote diversity in fundraising. It hopes the group will foster a greater understanding within the fundraising sector of multicultural giving.

Growth sectors

Increased pressure to diversify funding in the education, health and arts sectors has resulted in recent growth in fundraising activity.

Museums and galleries should develop a more 'entrepreneurial culture', according to a National Audit Office (NAO) report. Fundraising is already the major source of income for this sector but much of this activity is tied to specific campaigns and projects. Developing online services and products and investing in fundraising skills might help grow income, the report suggests.

Universities are being urged by government to set up dedicated fundraising or development offices. A government-commissioned task force says all universities should develop a professional approach to asking for money and improve relationships with alumni. Growth in fundraising by business schools is also expected.

Individual giving to the arts is estimated at around £236m, of which the large majority (73%) goes to London-based arts organisations. Arts & Business launched a programme in 2004 to increase public giving to the arts, particularly outside London and via tax-effective methods that are currently underutilised. It wants to see arts giving increase by £140m a year.

Changing demographics

One in three people in Britain is over 50 and by 2040 this group will account for half the population. An ageing population puts extra demands on health and social services so charities and voluntary organisations operating in these areas may need to increase fundraising in order to maintain services. This age group is estimated to have an annual spending power of around £240bn so there are also opportunities to attract older – and perhaps more wealthy – donors.

Mergers and joint working

Charity mergers and collaborations are changing the way many organisations approach fundraising. The recent merger of Cancer Research Campaign and Imperial Cancer Research Fund may have paved the way for other organisations looking for ways to improve service provision and reduce costs. Government and trust funders are particularly keen to see joint working feature as part of project bids.

Integration

Many organisations are finding that integrating the fundraising function with PR or communications helps to maximise the impact of their campaigns. This has resulted in fundraisers and press officers working together more closely. To make integration work, some organisations have merged departments or given an overarching remit to one director. At Age Concern, for example, the communications and marketing director counts fundraising, PR and policy in his remit.

Customised communication

An increasing number of fundraising organisations are looking at how they can 'personalise' relationships with donors. The thinking behind this is that all donors are different and have different needs at different times of their life. The fundraiser's job is to target their communications accordingly. Campaigning organisations have found that increasingly, donors want to be involved in campaign work; research into legacy prospects shows many do not want a relationship with the charity at all.

In 2004, WWF-UK replaced its fundraising function with a new 'supporter relationship management' department. Fundraising now includes better targeted mailings sent at a frequency specified by the supporter. The charity is also coordinating donor communications with its campaign work as supporters say they are keen to get involved in activities such as lobbying MPs.

Technology

Many charities are aware of the web's potential for generating income but few, if any, would agree that they are exploiting the opportunities sufficiently. Opportunities lie in integrating email and text messaging with fundraising activities and enhancing fundraising through technology such as online sponsorship forms. Using email to cultivate donors presents another opportunity.

The British Red Cross announced in 2004 that it is analysing donor patterns of behaviour on its website with a view to offering targeted or personalised email communications. There is also untapped potential for promoting products and services online.

Charities are currently testing the waters with interactive TV advertising, which presents a new opportunity for fundraisers to reach potential donors. British Red Cross and Barnardo's are among several to take part in an interactive TV trial on the Community Channel.

Income diversification

Falls in investments between 2000 and 2003 cut the value of charity investments by half, taking a significant chunk out of their reserves. Many have stepped up their fundraising efforts to plug the gaps or are looking at ways to diversify their income.

Increasing income through retail and trading operations is a popular choice. Victim Support's trading arm raised £75,000 in 2003 from selling training services to the retail and transport sector, and merchandise such as Christmas cards. The charity is hoping to grow income to £400,000 by 2009.

Cancer Research UK launched the first in a planned chain of high street card and gift shops in 2004. The Wishes chain will sell new products and shops will have more commercial feel than traditional charity shops. Oxfam is opening a chain of high street fair trade coffee shops, in a venture part-owned by growers' co-operatives in the developing world. The charity is also working with downloadable music firm OD2 to launch BigNoiseMusic.com – a website from which music fans will be able to download tracks, with 10p in every £1 spent going to Oxfam. And Dr B's, the Harrogate restaurant and coffee shop run by Barnardo's, earns income while helping to train underprivileged youngsters in the catering and hospitality industry.

The Charity Commission issued new guidance in 2004 urging charities to diversify their income to reduce risk of overdependence on one or two sources.

Jobs in fundraising

Introduction

Fundraising offers jobseekers a unique range of employers, jobs, career pathways and personal development opportunities. Ask fundraisers what they love most about working in the sector and you'll find that job satisfaction tops the list, but career advancement comes a close second. The growth of the not-for-profit sector in recent years has produced a raft of employment and training opportunities within charities and other fundraising organisations. And with salaries, benefits and working conditions to rival the private and public sectors, fundraising is now an attractive employment option for everyone from graduates and career switchers to job returners.

Sponsored events and street collections may be the familiar face of fundraising but a huge variety of skills and experiences lie behind this £14bn a year industry. As a fundraiser today, you're as likely to deal with blue-chip companies as with blue-rinse charity shop volunteers. You'll need to know about the law, managing volunteers and working with trustees. You'll also need strong interpersonal skills for your relationships with donors, funders and other partners. Above all, you need to be persistent and persuasive: in fundraising there are an awful lot of no's on the way to the yes's!

Depending on your skills and experience, there are opportunities to enter fundraising at almost every level and multiple routes to getting in. (See Section 4: Getting started.) In a small organisation, this may mean you are a general fundraiser working on your own to raise funds from a variety of sources. In larger organisations, you might be part of a fund-raising team or department, with responsibility for raising money from a specific source such as the lottery, grantmaking trusts or major donors.

Your specific tasks will depend on the organisation you work for but could include presenting sponsorship proposals to corporate donors; designing fundraising initiatives for schools or employee groups; co-ordinating the work of regional fundraisers; or managing commercial ventures such as charity shops.

Whichever organisation or job you choose, there are numerous opportunities to develop your fundraising skills. These include formal activities such as training and informal ones such as networking. Demand for fundraisers continues to rise in line with organisations' desire to diversify and increase their income, so it's an exciting and challenging time to enter the sector. And compared to marketing or media, the fundraising world is small enough for a talented fundraiser to get noticed quickly.

Why work in fundraising?

A passion for people and projects has always been at the heart of fundraisers' work. But the fundraising sector is now attracting entrants who are motivated by other considerations such as career development opportunities and flexible working hours.

For many fundraisers, the cause remains king. Over a third of Institute of Fundraising members surveyed in 2004 say affinity with their organisation's work is the main motivation for choosing their current job; one in 12 say their employer's reputation has attracted them to the position.

Worth noting however is that just under a quarter of those fundraisers surveyed say that career progression is behind their latest job move – an indication that fundraising is now regarded as a long-term employment option. And a significant number of fundraisers say that the chance to work part time, from home or as a consultant is the motivating factor for them.

Fundraisers' motivations for taking current job

Opportunities for career advancement	23.6%
Strong affinity with the cause	37.6%
Size of organisation	2.0%
Reputation of organisation	12.0%
Flexible working hours	2.2%
Self employment	2.7%
Location	3.8%
Other	16.1%

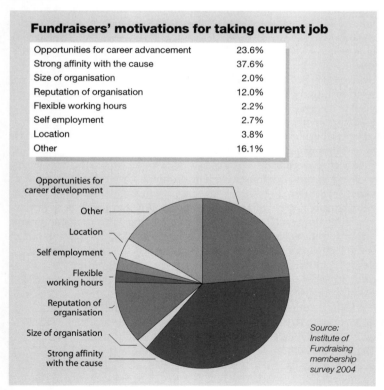

Source: Institute of Fundraising membership survey 2004

Here is a selection of fundraisers' comments on why they work where they do:

'A wish to make a contribution to life'

'Desire for a creative, challenging role'

'Commitment to the cause'

'Happiness at work'

'Varied workload'

'Enables me to influence outcomes'

'Wanted a change in direction'

'Huge job satisfaction'

'Lack of career advancement in previous post'

'Flexible working hours to juggle family and work'

'Job is close to home'

'Chance to be my own boss' (fundraising consultant)

As one director of fundraising says: 'Fundraising gives you the ability to change people's lives. How often can you say that about the business sector?'

About fundraisers

What do fundraisers do?

Fundraising jobs fall into four main categories, as defined by the 1992 Charities Act:

A *fundraiser* is a person who is directly employed by a charity to raise money for that organisation.

A *professional fundraiser* is someone directly involved in fundraising and who receives a financial reward in excess of £500 per annum for that activity.

A *volunteer fundraiser* is not remunerated for their fundraising work, but can be reimbursed for genuine out-of-pocket expenses. However, anyone receiving more than £5 per day or £500 per year total for direct fundraising work is considered to be a professional fundraiser and is therefore subject to the same legal regulations under the 1992 Charities Act.

A *consultant* is someone who is remunerated by a charity for fundraising work, including strategy and planning, but who does not become directly involved in asking donors for money.

❶▷ *Further information from the Charity Commission's website: www.charity-commission.gov.uk*

Budget responsibilities
The Institute's 2004 survey found that the large majority (71.5%) of fundraisers have personal responsibility for managing a budget. Nearly a quarter of respondents have a budget of between £100,000 and £249,000; 13% manage a budget of £1m or more.

Reporting and staff management
Whom you report to will depend on the level of your fundraising job, the size of the organisation you work for and its structure. You may report to a fundraising manager, non-fundraising senior manager, fundraising director or direct to your chief executive. Most of those responding to the Institute's survey report to their chief executive (28%) or fundraising director (17%). Around one in 10 fundraisers report to their trustees.

Annual budget managed by fundraisers

Budget responsibilities

Budget size	
Less than £10,000	8.1%
£10,000 to £29,999	9.5%
£30,000 to £49,999	7.4%
£50,000 to £99,999	12.9%
£100,000 to £249,999	24.0%
£250,000 to £499,999	15.9%
£500,000 to £999,999	9.4%
£1,000,000+	13.0%

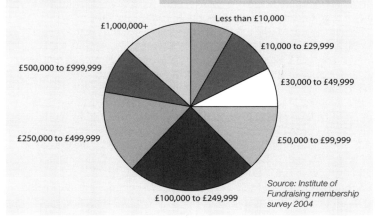

Source: Institute of Fundraising membership survey 2004

Number of employees managed by fundraisers

How many employees	
1 to 2	32.9%
3 to 4	25.6%
5 to 9	14.1%
10 to 19	12.4%
20 to 29	6.3%
30 to 39	1.5%
40 to 49	0.9%
50+	6.3%

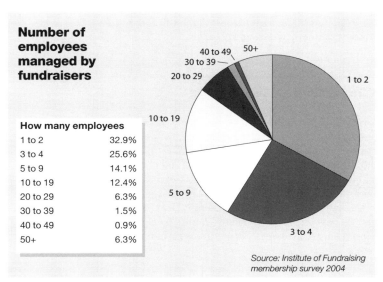

Source: Institute of Fundraising membership survey 2004

Over half (58%) of those surveyed have personal responsibility for other employees. Around a third of these manage one or two staff members and a quarter manage three or four. At the other end of the scale, 6.3% say they are responsible for 50 or more employees.

Who works in fundraising?

The Institute of Fundraising's 2004 membership survey found that just over two thirds of fundraisers (68%) are women and anecdotal evidence suggests that there is less of a 'glass ceiling' for women working in this sector than for those employed in the commercial sector.

The survey found that a third of fundraisers and the biggest single group are aged 25–34, reflecting the fact that many entrants to fundraising are 'second jobbers'. But this is a sector that also embraces the experience of age. Just over a fifth of fundraisers are aged 45–54 and more than one in 10 are 55–64 years old.

The majority of junior level posts (e.g. fundraising assistant or similar) and middle level jobs (e.g. fundraising manager) are held by fundraisers aged 25–34 years. Further up the fundraising ladder, senior level posts (e.g. head of fundraising department) are dominated by those aged 35–44 years – though it's worth noting that around 5% of senior jobs are held by those in the younger 25–34 years bracket.

Age does not appear to be a major barrier to getting a job at director level. Of the 218 fundraising directors surveyed, the largest single number (69) fall into the 45–54 years bracket. However, a similar number (65) are aged 35–44 years while slightly fewer (54) are aged 55–64 years. And a small number (25) of fundraisers in the 25–34 years bracket currently work at director level.

Where do they work?

Fundraisers work in a wide variety of organisations, from arts centres and hospices to political parties and universities. However, the majority of fundraising jobs are to be found in charities and voluntary organisations, where public donations and grants account for a significant proportion of income. The Institute's 2004 survey shows that medical organisations employ the single largest number of fundraisers; organisations working in the disability field, with children and in health are the next biggest employers. Around 7% of those surveyed work as fundraising consultants, either through a consultancy or on a freelance basis.

Fundraising roles by age

Age	18–24	25–34	35–44	45–54	55–64	65+
Director level	0.0%	6.6%	21.5%	26.5%	36.70%	33.30%
Senior level	5.0%	15.1%	25.2%	20.4%	19.00%	6.70%
Middle level	40.0%	55.7%	33.1%	28.8%	19.00%	13.30%
Junior level	45.0%	10.9%	3.3%	2.3%	0.00%	0.00%
Other	10.0%	11.7%	16.9%	21.9%	25.20%	46.70%

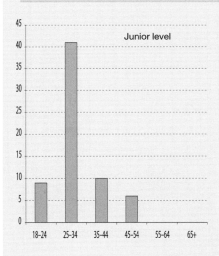

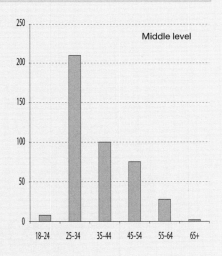

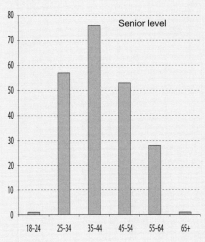

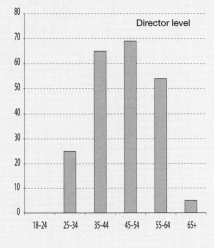

Source: Institute of Fundraising membership survey 2004

What sort of organisations do fundraisers work for?

Organisation			
Health	7.60%	Homelessness	2.30%
Medical	12.30%	Arts	2.90%
Children	9.50%	Education	6.40%
Disability	10.90%	International aid	5.90%
Animal welfare	1.90%	Benevolent funds	0.90%
Social welfare	6.10%	Environment	3.80%
Elderly	3.00%	Crime	0.60%
Human rights	0.60%	Faith	2.70%
Culture & heritage	1.90%	Peace	0.10%
		Other	20.70%

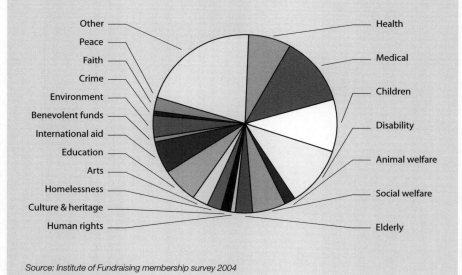

Source: Institute of Fundraising membership survey 2004

Where are they located?

London and the south east dominate the employment market for fundraisers: almost a third of Institute members say they work in the capital while one in seven is based in the south east. This reflects the fact that a large number of charities and voluntary organisations have their headquarters in these areas, although many also have regional offices where fundraisers work.

High numbers of fundraisers are also to be found in Scotland and the south west. Around 1% of those surveyed are based outside the UK, mostly in Europe. The remaining jobs are to be found in the regions, typically in local charities or local branches of national charities.

ⓘ See **Section 3** *for information about fundraising salaries and benefits*

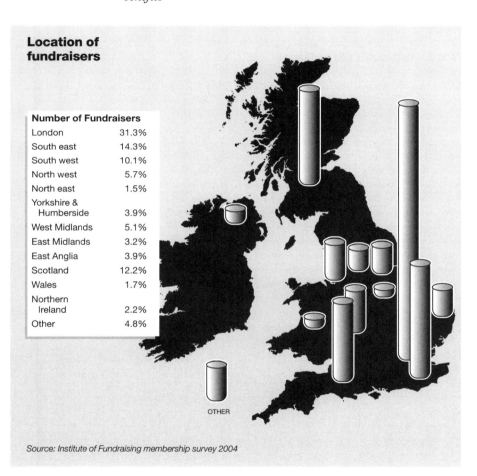

Location of fundraisers

Number of Fundraisers	
London	31.3%
South east	14.3%
South west	10.1%
North west	5.7%
North east	1.5%
Yorkshire & Humberside	3.9%
West Midlands	5.1%
East Midlands	3.2%
East Anglia	3.9%
Scotland	12.2%
Wales	1.7%
Northern Ireland	2.2%
Other	4.8%

OTHER

Source: Institute of Fundraising membership survey 2004

About fundraising jobs

Organisational structure

The remit of your job in fundraising will depend on the size and nature of the organisation you work for. A large charity may have 30 or more fundraisers working in its fundraising department, with separate teams for events, corporate, legacies, trusts and other specialisms. A small organisation such as a hospice or school may have just one fundraiser who is responsible for securing donations through a variety of means.

Your fundraising job may be positioned within a standalone fundraising department or a joint fundraising and marketing department. Alternatively it may be in a fundraising team that is part of a larger department, such as development or communications.

In larger organisations, a head of fundraising or director of fundraising will lead your team or department. In a smaller one, you may report directly to the chief executive and/or a member of the trustee board who has been allocated responsibility for fundraising. Your organisation may also have a fundraising sub-committee that reports to the main trustee board.

Roles

There is no single career pathway in fundraising, particularly as such a high proportion of fundraisers join from other sectors and transfer their skills to the job.

Broadly speaking, if you have limited work experience or skills you might join the sector as a *volunteer fundraiser* or *fundraising assistant*. This role may involve assisting a fundraiser or supporting the fundraising team.

If you are a graduate or have relevant skills such as research analysis or proposal writing, you might find a job as a *general, specialist* or *freelance fundraiser*.

Proven sector experience and professional development should enable you to work as a *senior fundraiser* (or *head of fundraising* in a smaller organisation). In the commercial sector (see sections on **Consultancy**

work and **Service providers and agencies** below), this experience might help you to get a job as a *brand manager, database manager, direct marketing manager* or *e-marketing manager.*

Extensive sector experience combined with management, leadership and business skills will equip you to work as a *head of fundraising* in a larger organisation or as a *senior fundraising specialist.* Your next step may then be to a *chief executive* role, either in a fundraising organisation or commercial consultancy.

Some or all of these roles may also include an element of marketing, PR or communications work. For instance, as a fundraiser you may also have responsibility for an organisation's annual report or dealing with the media. The level to which this occurs will depend on the size and structure of your organisation.

❶ *See* **Section 4** *and* **Section 5** *for more information about job hunting and career development*

Consultancy work

Fundraising consultants help organisations to fill the gaps in their experience and to exploit their potential. Consultants work as individuals or through a consultancy to offer specialist expertise and objective advice. Some fundraising organisations may use consultants for one-off projects, where they need expertise without the extra overheads associated with staff. Others may retain a consultant or agency to advise on fundraising strategy.

Typical activities include:

- reviewing a fundraising strategy
- advising on a one-off project, e.g. a new capital campaign or endowment fund
- identifying new donors
- developing new income streams

An increasing number of fundraisers are 'crossing the fence' to use the skills and knowledge acquired within fundraising organisations in a consultancy capacity. Consultancy work offers the advantages of working with a variety of causes or fundraising sectors and on time-limited projects. However, some 'switchers' say they miss working for a single cause or in the not-for-profit environment.

Service providers and agencies

Many fundraising organisations use specialist service providers and agencies in their work. These companies may specialise in:

- database management
- direct marketing
- face-to-face fundraising

- market research
- payroll giving
- telemarketing
- website design

These companies offer another opportunity for potential and experienced fundraisers to use their skills, in areas such as IT, marketing, sales and research. Often work activities are similar to those in fundraising organisations (see **Typical work activities**, below). There may be a high level of contact with the client organisation.

A comprehensive listing of service providers, agencies and fundraising consultants appears in Who's Who in Fundraising, published each year by the Institute of Fundraising.

ⓘ *See* **Directory** *for further information about Who's Who in Fundraising*

ⓘ *See* **Section 4** *for details of where to look for job vacancies*

Specialist or generalist?

Whether your job in fundraising requires specialist or general skills depends on a variety of factors. One is the size of the organisation you work for: a large fundraising organisation such as a national charity will have opportunities to specialise in particular techniques; a smaller one might expect you to be a Jack or Jill of all trades.

Sector spotlight: Direct marketing

Direct marketing is one of the most established areas of fundraising and uses methods such as direct mail, telemarketing, radio/TV appeals and press advertising. Many fundraising organisations use direct marketing agencies to help them devise and execute their campaigns.

Graduate recruitment schemes aren't widespread in agencies, although a few say that they take on graduate trainees on an ad hoc basis. More commonly, entrants will have a sales or marketing background gained in the commercial sector or will come from a similar role in the voluntary sector. With little experience, you may enter an agency in a junior position such as account executive or manager. Those with more experience may join as senior account manager or director. An experienced fundraiser or marketer could go in as group account director.

Activities include planning and implementing campaigns; working out budgets; working with creative and media planning teams and liaising closely with the client. Agencies look for good project management skills; ability to work with clients and in-house contacts and strong interpersonal skills.

Another is the nature of your organisation's work: a university hospital for example may be heavily dependent on grantmaking trusts and company donations but have limited appeal to individual donors. As such, its fundraiser or fundraising team would be expected to have specialist experience in trust fundraising or corporate fundraising.

Large organisations offer you the chance to develop more specialist skills and develop in-depth knowledge of your fundraising technique. In smaller organisations, there is greater exposure to different areas of work which adds variety to the role.

ⓘ *See* **Section 5** *for more on specialising vs generalising*

Personal skills needed

Different donors have different needs at different stages of their lives. As a fundraiser your job is to understand and meet those needs. To do this requires:

Good communications skills

Fundraisers must be able to explain often quite complex issues to donors, potential donors, sponsors and other partners. You'll need to convey what it is that is so special about your organisation's work, who benefits from it and why this work needs to continue. This may be in person, on the telephone or through written communications. Good relationships with contacts are a vital part of fundraising.

Good organisational and planning skills

Recruiting and retaining donors requires a systematic approach. You'll need to plan approaches and campaigns; maintain donor databases; update records and keep files on correspondence.

Ability to think laterally

Potential funders are everywhere – your job as a fundraiser is to find them. Often this means looking beyond the 'obvious' sources of funding to find untapped income streams or donor groups. For example, asking a company to encourage employees to volunteer their time for your organisation may meet with more success than asking for a cash donation. It also involves making connections: a celebrity who mentions in an interview that a close family member has AIDS might want to support your HIV charity.

Creativity

Successful fundraising relies on finding imaginative and innovative ways to engage with existing and potential donors, funders and other partners. This may involve researching and executing new fundraising techniques, such as use of the internet or special events.

Powers of persuasion

Donors and funders have a million and one demands on their money and time. Why should they give either to your charity, school, theatre or church? You'll need to be able to make the case for your organisation, through compelling arguments and persuasive correspondence. And once you've got their interest, you'll need to maintain it by letting them know how their donation is helping and what continued support can achieve.

Commitment to/enthusiasm for the cause

A passion for the people and projects your organisation supports will help you convey the significance of the work to your donors. You're unlikely to win their time or money if you can't muster any enthusiasm for the cause. Rejection is a part of fundraising life so commitment to your organisation's work will also help you to deal with the no's.

Persistence

Even the most successful fundraiser will encounter the word No en route to a Yes. You'll need to be thick skinned and take these knock-backs in your stride. Rejections can help you to hone your fundraising skills so that the 'ask' becomes easier.

Personal perspective: Lucy Phillips

Job: Corporate relations manager

Organisation: Home-Start

Age: 34

It was by fluke, rather than a planned career choice, that I ended up in fundraising eight years ago when I applied for the post of regional appeals committee executive at deafblind charity Sense, advertised in the Guardian. But it's by choice that I stayed in fundraising and am now corporate relations manager for Home-Start, which helps families who are struggling to cope with young children.

I work for the organisation's central office in Leicester, and we provide training, guidance and policy for local schemes. There are over 330 Home-Start schemes across the country, each are registered charities run by committees of local volunteers with at least one paid worker who recruits and trains volunteers to support families. Some schemes receive all their funding from local authorities but others don't get much – it really varies.

As corporate relations manager, I am responsible for overseeing company partnerships with a number of organisations including: a three-year £750,000 grant from the Vodafone UK Foundation; employee fundraising and volunteering schemes with the Woolworths Kids First charity arm of the high street retailer, and a three-year sponsorship deal with the Tesco Baby and Toddler club.

Five years of commercial marketing experience gained at the Exhibition Team, where I eventually became operations manager before moving into fundraising, has proved valuable when dealing with corporates. As have Chartered Institute of Marketing qualifications gained during my time as a senior fundraising adviser for the Abbeyfield Society, provider of housing with care for older people. It allows me to use the right language and a relevant approach.

Being home-based for half the week allows me to write reports and funding applications away from the distractions of the office. But I also enjoy brainstorming with my colleagues, including the two other fundraisers working to achieve the £1.2m voluntary income needed each year. We enjoy it and have a laugh too!

Typical work activities

Your job in fundraising may cover some or all of the following activities:

- developing new income streams, e.g. internet fundraising and online auctions
- organising and promoting events
- developing and maintaining relationships with donors/potential donors
- writing campaign materials
- working with the media to promote activities and develop fundraising opportunities
- maintaining donor databases
- recruiting and working with volunteers, e.g. in charity shops or at sponsored events
- researching new sources of funding, e.g. charitable trusts, corporate donations, lottery funding.

Fundraising national occupational standards (NOS)

The fundraising national occupational standards (NOS) have been developed by the Voluntary Sector National Training Organisation (VSNTO) in association with the fundraising sector to demonstrate what effective fundraising entails.

The standards are designed to enable those who work to raise funds and resources – both paid and unpaid – to demonstrate and enhance their skills. Eventually they will form the basis of S/NVQs at levels 2, 3 and 4 for managing fundraising.

The three levels of standards set out the knowledge and understanding required to perform tasks such as:

- assisting with fundraising activities
- contributing to the maintenance of relationships with supporters
- assisting with fundraising plans
- processing financial information
- using IT to support fundraising
- conducting risk assessments for fundraising activities

ⓘ▸ *Further information about the fundraising NOS from www.voluntarysectorskills.org.uk*

Here are some examples of the work activities included in common fundraising jobs and the key skills needed:

Big gift fundraiser

- Researching prospective wealthy donors
- Developing a relationship with supporters
- Organising profile-raising events
- Liaising with current givers who may convert to big givers

Key skills: Excellent relationship-building skills are needed in this job as you need to win the donor's trust before you ask them for a significant donation. You'll also need good presentation skills and feel comfortable dealing with people at a one-to-one level. The ability to make and develop contacts is also important.

Community fundraiser

- Working across a range of fundraising disciplines, from charity shops to challenge events
- Recruiting, training and supporting volunteers
- Approaching local companies, schools, membership organisations, Rotary clubs and so on for support
- Approaching grantmaking organisations and trusts
- Raising awareness of activities through the local press, talks, regional publications etc

Key skills: Planning and organisational skills are vital as you'll need to keep track of a number of fundraising activities. Budgeting skills are also useful as community fundraisers usually have responsibility for their own budget for local or regional work. Marketing and PR skills will help you to publicise activities and spot media opportunities. You should also be a good people manager as much of your time will involve co-ordinating the work of volunteers and keeping them motivated.

Corporate fundraiser

- Liaising with companies on initiatives such as payroll giving and employee volunteering
- Managing charity of the year relationships
- Devising cause-related marketing strategies
- Arranging sponsorship deals
- Securing large donations

Key skills: Good research skills are essential as you'll need to find out who makes the decisions in the company, what they support, how they are structured, how many employees they have and how the business is performing. Communication and presentation skills are also important as you'll need to 'sell' your proposal to the company. Negotiation skills will be useful as you'll need to work with the company to ensure the relationship is of mutual benefit.

Development manager

- Writing to alumni
- Developing relationships with local companies
- Setting up membership deals
- Co-ordinating capital campaigns

Key skills: You'll need good research skills to keep tabs on what past students are doing and organisational skills to maintain a database of current and potential donors. Opportunism is also important: you need to be able to spot a potential relationship with a local funder or high-profile alumnus.

Legacy fundraiser

- Developing relationships with supporters to encourage them to leave a legacy to your organisation
- Researching potential high value donors
- Liaising with local volunteer fundraisers
- Working with solicitors to promote legacies

Key skills: Diplomacy and good relationship building skills are key to this job. You need to be good with people, sensitive to family environments and have a broad understanding of why people support charities. Good written communication skills will help if your organisation uses direct marketing for its legacy campaigns. You'll also need good communication skills as legacy recruitment is often done through face-to-face visits.

Retail manager

- Developing branding of shop fronts and merchandise
- Planning new shop locations and shop closures
- Managing staff and volunteers
- Liaising with suppliers of bought-in stock
- Working with companies to secure donated goods

Key skills: Sales and marketing skills are central to this role and you'll need to be creative in order for your brand to stand out from the crowd. You'll also need good people management skills: trading activities often rely on volunteers to manage them and your job is to keep them motivated and reward their loyalty.

Trading manager

- Selecting products for sale through shops or catalogues
- Devising a marketing strategy for products or services
- Working with local fundraising committees to promote products
- Liaising with commercial partners on cause related marketing products or services

Key skills: For this role, you'll need sound business skills including dealing with accounts and budgeting. Sales and marketing skills are essential, as is the ability to think laterally and spot potential relationships with the commercial sector.

Trust and grant fundraiser

- Desk-based research of databases, grantmaking guides etc
- Writing funding applications
- Liaising with service providers within the charity to build up the case for support and develop relationships with potential donors

Key skills: Research skills are vital for this role as you'll spend much of your time trawling through directories, the internet, library resources and networks for potential funding. Excellent written skills are needed to put together funding proposals and complete application forms. You'll need to be able to 'match' your work to the funder's criteria and explain clearly why they should give. Attention to detail is paramount as funders have strict criteria about whom they will fund.

ⓘ▷ *See* **Section 1** *for more information on different fundraising techniques*

Fundraising focus: Hospice fundraising

The fundraising message is clear for the Ayrshire Hospice in south west Scotland – your £1 helps provide care in your local community. 'Everyone knows a colleague, family friend or neighbour who has used the hospice and it has an excellent reputation,' says fundraising manager Louis Jardine. As well as providing care for people with advanced cancer and motor neurone disease, the hospice also offers an education programme in cancer and palliative care.

As GPs and consultants make more referrals to the hospice, it comes under increasing pressure to reach its fundraising target of at least £3.4m a year. Just over £1m is statutory funding from the local health authority and the remainder is down to a fundraising team of nine paid staff and five charity shops, helped by an army of volunteers.

The strong community support for the hospice helps to boost proceeds for its largest source of voluntary income – a local lottery. Jardine started the game from scratch but it now brings in £685,000 annually. Hospice representatives collect £1 a week from 14,000 people in the local area who hope to win prizes worth £3,000, while profits go directly to the hospice. The fact that the hospice, rather than a third profit-making party, runs the lottery itself helps to encourage local participation, believes Jardine.

A balanced approach to fundraising, while keeping a close eye on the costs involved, is essential, according to Jardine. The hospice raises the rest of its income through community events, charity shops, a friends network, the education centre, investments, general donations, legacies and money from grantmaking trusts.

Sample job vacancies

The following vacancies were advertised in the Guardian during 2004 and show the range of job opportunities and skills needed in fundraising.

Organisation	Heritage trust
Job	Fundraiser
Location	South west
Annual salary	£16,000–£24,000
Key tasks	Helping to raise £1m for conservation project
Skills/experience required	Proven track record of raising funds from companies, trusts and public

Organisation	University – development office
Job	Assistant annual giving officer
Location	Midlands
Annual salary	£16,942–£24,155
Key tasks	Planning and implementing annual giving programme
	Telephone fundraising and direct mail campaigns to former students
	Assistance with staff recruitment, training and supervision
Skills/experience required	A Level or equivalent qualification
	GCSEs in English and mathematics at Grade C or above (or equivalent)
	Minimum of three years' experience in a similar role
	Experience of supervising teams
	Good computing and IT skills
	Ability to utilise reports and statistics

Organisation	Overseas aid charity
Job	Corporate partnerships executive
Location	London
Annual salary	£19,000–£24,000
Key tasks	Fundraising with UK and international companies
Skills/experience required	Account management
	New business development
	Degree or equivalent
	Minimum of two years experience in a fundraising, marketing or sales role, including account management
	Project management

Organisation	Arts centre
Job	Fundraising manager
Location	North west
Annual salary	£20,000–£24,000
Key tasks	Implementing fundraising strategy
Skills/experience required	Understanding of different funding sectors
	Exceptional communication, negotiation and networking skills
	Strong media focus

Organisation	Adoption charity
Job	Trusts fundraising manager
Location	London
Annual salary	£35,467–£40,904
Key tasks	Securing donations from grantmaking trusts
Skills/experience required	Proven success in trust fundraising
	Excellent proposal writing, planning and research skills

Organisation	Crime reduction charity
Job	Fundraising & marketing officer
Location	South east
Annual salary	£22,550–£26,650
Key tasks	Building relationships with supporters in the statutory, business and charity sectors
Skills/experience required	Previous experience as a fundraiser or marketer
	Research & information gathering skills to spot funding opportunities
	Persuasive copywriting, interpersonal and presentation skills

Organisation	Independent school
Job	Fundraiser
Location	Midlands
Annual salary	£25,000
Key tasks	Expanding fundraising strategy for new school development
Skills/experience required	Schools fundraising experience Knowledge of Raiser's Edge (software)
	Strong communication and interpersonal skills

Organisation	NHS trust
Job	Fundraising director
Location	London
Annual salary	£60,000 plus PRP
Key tasks	Developing and implementing a capital and revenue fundraising strategy Preparing income and expenditure budgets
	Enhancing network of senior volunteers
Skills/experience required	Appreciation of NHS/other healthcare policies Knowledge of sponsorship environment

Sample job description and person specification: fundraising manager

Responsible to   Director of fundraising

Department   Fundraising

Main purpose of job   To maximise the generation of funds for XYZ charity

Duties

- generate increased income from existing sources
- identify and research potential funding opportunities
- develop proposals for projects that could attract new funding
- establish links with other voluntary and statutory bodies
- assist director in developing a three-year fundraising strategy
- liaise with press officer for profile raising events

Role

Your job is to access funds to enable the continuing work of XYZ in its role as a provider of care facilities for vulnerable people. You will be responsible for all fundraising activity, conducted on behalf of the organisation. As fundraising manager you will also be expected to lead the fundraising team and oversee the management and development of three fundraising officers. As a member of the management team you will be expected to contribute to long-term planning and attend monthly management team meetings.

Person specification

Essential skills/ abilities   Generation of creative ideas, good communication skills (written and oral) Computer literacy, management skills

Desirable   Use of Excel

Essential knowledge   Knowledge of fundraising and funding

Desirable   Knowledge of voluntary care sector, knowledge of management techniques

Source: NVQ

ⓘ *For more job descriptions and person specifications, see* **Section 4**

Fundraising focus: BME fundraising

Help the Aged is one of the organisations currently forging ahead with fundraising in black and minority ethnic (BME) communities. The charity, which provides services and campaigns to uphold the rights of older people, is working closely with British Asians to encourage them to support their communities by volunteering, fundraising, raising awareness and attending events. And working in partnership with organisations in India, Sri Lanka and Bangladesh, Help the Aged directly supports projects in South Asia, with schemes like Adopt A Granny and Mobile Medicare.

Deepa Patel was appointed as the charity's first international development manager to take this work forward. Her background as a lawyer and government consultant, combined with an ability to speak three different Indian languages, were just some of the reasons she was headhunted for this post.

'You need a specialist knowledge of different cultures so that you are aware and respectful. You have to build up the trust and minorities often want to see someone representative of their community,' explains Patel.

Her role is three-pronged. She works with older people in Indian communities in the UK to help identify their specific needs and encourage them to use Help the Aged services. She is also developing support from the charity's network of Chakra Patrons – a group of prominent community leaders in the regions. Glasgow, Manchester, the east Midlands and the west Midlands all have Chakra Patrons and there are two based in London.

Raising the profile of the charity through the Asian Business Awards, where Help the Aged was chosen as charity of the year as a result of its work in India, is another key part of Patel's role. Through initiatives like this, she hopes to bring more Indian business professionals across the world on board, pointing out that BME businesses make a £41bn contribution to the global economy. 'This will help ensure that this work has an even deeper and more sustainable impact,' she adds.

BME fundraising is likely to become even more event focused in the future to tie in with many of the celebrations held in BME communities, according to Patel. In addition to the business connections, much of her fundraising is currently conducted through small networking events where she talks about particular projects and puts forward proposals when appropriate. Some British Asian donors have decided to fund Mobile Medicare units based in the area of India where their families came from originally, for example.

She says the fundraising projects help to present people from BME communities in a positive light. 'There is still a lot of prejudice out there and the media often presents negative aspects, like deprivation and crime. But we are looking at positive factors and encouraging people from diverse backgrounds to support their communities.'

Fundraising focus: Community fundraising

Marie Curie Cancer Care provides free care to around 30,000 cancer patients and their families each year, caring for patients either in their own homes or at one of its 10 hospices. To do this, the charity raises £50m annually in voluntary income and the regional fundraising team, which includes the community fundraisers, raises £18m of that.

Marie Curie has a team of 200 full-time fundraisers but it also relies heavily on more than 5,000 volunteers and most of them are involved in its community fundraising programme. The charity estimates that the time given and talent offered by those volunteers, is worth around £5m a year. Many decide to volunteer after receiving help from the charity for themselves or a family member.

Community fundraisers provide the 'face' of Marie Curie and respond to individual donors, according to its fundraising director, Sandra Osbourne. They are involved in a wide range of activities from organising traditional coffee mornings and jumble sales to abseils and photo calls for the local press. They also organise employee volunteering programmes and street collections for the charity's annual national daffodil fundraising campaign, amongst many other things.

'There's a tendency to think that overseas events is the most exciting area of fundraising but you can do some event management in a community fundraising role, along with lots of elements of the other roles too,' adds Osbourne. And she is speaking from experience – after 14 years as a nurse working with adults with head injuries, Osbourne joined Scope (then called the Spastics Society), as a community fundraiser. Experience gained as a volunteer fundraiser for her children's schools definitely helped Osbourne to get the job.

Communication skills, optimism and determination are required for community fundraising, according to Osbourne. And all were needed when the charity's daffodil campaign was hit hard by the foot and mouth crisis. A fundraising run was cancelled and volunteers in rural areas could not go out to gather collections.

'Sometimes things happen that are just beyond your control,' says Osbourne. 'It is disappointing but the nice thing about community fundraising is that it is made up of so many different things that you never have to wait long before another opportunity presents itself. And if I'm ever having a hard day, I just read one of the letters sent by people telling us what a difference Marie Curie made to them and it reminds me what we're here for.'

Salaries, benefits & working conditions

Introduction

Increasingly competitive salaries, flexible working conditions and opportunities for varied job progression make fundraising an attractive career choice. Once thought of as a Cinderella sector compared to related disciplines such as marketing or sales, fundraising has professionalised to offer a range of benefits to people at all stages of their career.

Conditions of employment vary from organisation to organisation and depend on a variety of factors. These include the type of fundraising practised: for example, some fundraisers use a variety of techniques to plan for short-, medium- and long-term income generation; others employ specialist skills. Factors could also include the region in which your job is based, the size and income of the fundraising organisation you work for and your level of responsibility.

Employers in the voluntary sector often offer excellent benefits such as flexible working, training and career development opportunities and even time off for volunteering. So it is important that you look at the total reward package and not just the salary offered.

The 2003 Annual Voluntary Sector Salary Survey shows that the average pay award in the year to July 2003 was 3.1%, which is in line with the average earnings index (3.2%) and retail price index (3.1%). The survey, compiled by Remuneration Economics in association with the National Council for Voluntary Organisations (NCVO), also found that average salaries of women working in the sector increased at a higher rate than those of their male counterparts over the survey period. A 2003 survey by IRS Employment Review found that several charities including Blue Cross and Heritage Care now directly link staff pay rises with the retail price index.

The Institute of Fundraising's 2004 membership survey shows that almost the same number of people increased their salary on entering fundraising as took a pay cut. It's inevitable that fundraising organisations will be cost conscious, as they want to get the most out of each donor pound. But given the perennial problem of finding new donors and retaining existing ones, many organisations have succeeded in persuading their trustees that significant investment in fundraising – including good staff – will reap rewards.

Salaries in fundraising

How much do fundraisers earn?

Fundraising salaries vary considerably from one organisation to another. Many are subject to regional variations or directly related to the size of an organisation's voluntary income.

While salaries in this sector will not always reflect the pay for equivalent jobs in the private sector, increased professionalism and the prevalence of career 'switchers' have driven them up in recent years, particularly at more senior levels.

The Institute's 2004 survey found that fundraisers currently earn anything from under £10,000 to over £100,000. Gross annual salaries of between £20,000 and £29,000 are the most prevalent, with just under 45% of fundraisers falling into this income band. Just over a fifth (21%) earn between £30,000 and £39,000 a year; almost one in 10 earns between £40,000 and £49,000. Overall, 17% of fundraisers have a salary of £40,000 or more, with 2% earning over £60,000.

Although many people take a pay cut to enter fundraising, this is not always the case. While a third (38%) were earning more money before taking a job in fundraising, a similar number – 36% – were on a lower salary while 16% moved into the sector on the same wage. The majority (56%) of respondents moved into fundraising on a salary of between £10,000 and £19,999.

Director level e.g. director of fundraising
Almost a third (31%) of fundraising directors surveyed earn between £30,000 and £39,999. Around a fifth (21%) are paid between £40,000 and £49,999. Only 1% of respondents – two directors – received less than £10,000.

Senior level e.g. head of department
At this level, 39% are paid between £30,000 and £39,999 and 37.5% are on £20,000–£29,999. Fewer than 1% – only one person – earn under £10,000.

Annual gross salary of fundraisers

Less than £10,000	20	1.8%	£60,000 – £69,999	13	1.2%
£10,000 – £19,999	143	12.8%	£70,000 – £79,999	15	1.3%
£20,000 – £29,999	500	44.6%	£80,000 – £89,999	5	0.4%
£30,000 – £39,999	237	21.1%	£90,000 – £99,999	2	0.2%
£40,000 – £49,999	107	9.5%	£100,000+	4	0.4%
£50,000 – £59,999	43	3.8%	I'd prefer not to say	32	2.9%

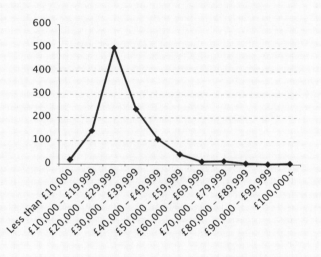

Source: Institute of Fundraising membership survey 2004

Middle level e.g. fundraising manager

The vast majority – some 70% – earn between £20,000 and £29,999. The next biggest group – some 14% – are paid between £10,000 and £19,999. Just 1% – four managers – earn less than £10,000.

Junior level e.g. fundraising assistant

Most people (59%) working at this level are paid between £10,000 and £19,999. Another 36% earn more – between £20,000 and £29,999. At this level, lower salaries are more common with 3% of junior fundraisers earning less than £10,000.

Salary by job title

Gross annual salary?	Director level (e.g. director of fundraising)		Senior level (e.g. head of department)		Middle level (e.g. fundraising manager)		Junior level (e.g. fundraising assistant)	
Less than £10,000	2	0.9%	1	0.5%	4	0.9%	2	3.0%
£10,000 – £19,999	6	2.8%	8	3.7%	58	13.7%	39	59.1%
£20,000 – £29,999	35	16.1%	81	37.5%	297	70.2%	24	36.4%
£30,000 – £39,999	67	30.7%	84	38.9%	55	13.0%	0	0.0%
£40,000 – £49,999	46	21.1%	36	16.7%	5	1.2%	0	0.0%
£50,000 – £59,999	31	14.2%	1	0.5%	0	0.0%	0	0.0%
£60,000 – £69,999	7	3.2%	2	0.9%	1	0.2%	0	0.0%
£70,000 – £79,999	9	4.1%	0	0.0%	0	0.0%	0	0.0%
£80,000 – £89,999	4	1.8%	0	0.0%	0	0.0%	0	0.0%
£90,000 – £99,999	1	0.5%	0	0.0%	0	0.0%	0	0.0%
£100,000+	2	0.9%	0	0.0%	0	0.0%	0	0.0%
I'd prefer not to say	8	3.7%	3	1.4%	3	0.7%	1	1.5%
Total	218	100.0%	216	100.0%	423	100.0%	66	100.0%

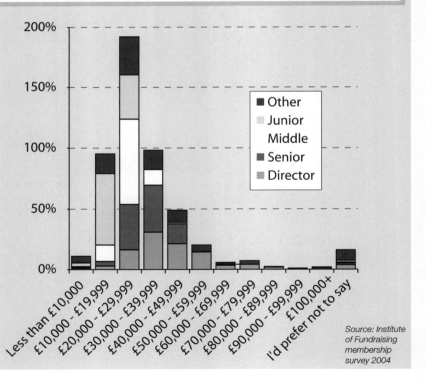

Source: Institute of Fundraising membership survey 2004

Salaries and size of organisation

Not surprisingly, fundraising salaries are closely connected with the income of the organisation. Findings from the 2003 Annual Voluntary Sector Salary Survey by Remuneration Economics shows that the average salary for a director or head of fundraising in a charity with an income of less than £3m was around £34,603 – compared to £45,587 for the same position in a charity with income of between £10m and £25m, and £68,340 for a similar job in a charity with income of over £25m. The differential is less noticeable when you compare salaries for more junior positions. Specialist staff in a charity with income of less than £3m receive an average £21,911, compared to £22,981 in a charity with income of between £10m and £25m and £27,926 in a charity with income of £25m plus.

The Institute survey shows that, by and large, salary levels are related to the size of the organisation. One in 10 fundraisers working for charities raising £20m or more, and 15% of those with a voluntary income target of between £10m and £19m, earns over £50,000. However, salaries of between £20,000 and £29,000 account for the largest part of charities' wage bill across the board, ranging from 34% in organisations with voluntary income of less than £10,000 to 53% in those raising £10m plus.

Regional variations

Fundraisers in London and the south east are more likely than their regional counterparts to be high earners. While 11% of fundraisers in the capital and 10% in the south east earn £50,000 or more, only the north west and Scotland are similarly generous – though only 5% of fundraiser in each region top the £50,000 mark. It is worth noting that salaries of £100,000 plus are not confined to the south east, showing up in the north east and Yorkshire & Humberside but not in London.

Salaries in London

Average salaries in London have increased in most job categories in the past year, according to research by fundraising recruitment agency the Kage Partnership. Its fifth annual survey of advertised salaries for vacancies in over 130 London charities shows that salaries are up on previous years, reflecting annual pay reviews as would be expected in most organisations. However, the wide range of salaries advertised reflects the disparity in pay between organisations in the sector.

Fundraising salaries in London

Job type	£ Average salary*
Junior	
Fundraising assistant	18,000
Officer/executive/senior executive	
Corporate fundraiser	23,000
Trust/major donor fundraiser	23,000
Events fundraiser	22,500
Community/regional fundraiser	21,500
Direct marketing executive	22,000
Communications executive	24,000
Manager	
Corporate fundraising manager	31,000
Trust/major donor fundraising manager	29,000
Events fundraising manager	29,000
Community fundraising manager	31,500
Direct marketing manager	31,000
Communications manager	31,500
Senior	
Director/head of fundraising or communications (small- or medium-sized organisations)	38,500

*All salaries include London weighting

Source: The Kage Partnership Fundraising Salary Report 2004

Performance-related pay

Competition for funds combined with the need to recruit and retain good staff has seen emergence of performance-related pay in the fundraising sector over the last 10 years. PRP is particularly prevalent in target-focused work such as face-to-face fundraising, where for example a guaranteed minimum salary of £190 per week may rise to between £250 and £350 per week depending on performance. However, the practice of merit-related pay is spreading to other parts of the fundraising sector.

A survey of 26 charities conducted by IRS Employment Review in 2003 found that 11 employers incorporated performance-related pay to some extent. Of these, five awarded rises based solely on merit – a strategy that none of the employers surveyed the previous year had adopted.

The survey covered approximately 67,000 employees – around 10% of the national voluntary sector workforce. The findings indicate that voluntary organisations are becoming more responsive to market drivers and sector commentators expect individual performance-related pay to become widespread. Indeed, a 2003 survey conducted by the Association of Chief Executives of Voluntary Organisations (ACEVO) shows that just under a third (30.7%) of charity chiefs who are appraised have their salaries based on that appraisal.

Finding out more

To gain a better understanding of appropriate salary levels, look at job advertisements in the sector press, on recruitment websites and in local newspapers. It is also worth contacting recruitment consultants who will be able to give you an idea of market rates and may have information on salary trends based on region or fundraising function.

Salary surveys

There are several regular surveys of salaries in the voluntary sector and in fundraising. While these are produced primarily for organisations and therefore sold at a premium rate, individuals can glean information from coverage in the trade press or survey highlights on the publishers' websites. These include:

- Annual Voluntary Sector Salary Survey: yearly snapshot of charity salaries produced by Remuneration Economics in association with the National Council of Voluntary Organisations. Details: www.celre.co.uk

- Charity Rewards: annual survey of salaries and benefits in the not-for-profit sector. Produced by Croner Reward in association with Charity and Fundraising Appointments and the Charity Finance Directors Group. Details: www.croner-reward.co.uk

- Fundraising Salary Survey: Annual survey of fundraising salaries produced by fundraising recruitment consultancy, Kage Partnership. Details: www.kagep.com

❶» *See* Directory *for full contact details*

Fundraising focus: Big gifts

Big gift (or major donor) fundraising involves large, one-off donations, which are given to a charity to support a specific programme.

Paul Collins, director of fundraising at the Simon Community Northern Ireland (SCNI), managed a big gift appeal to raise £300,000 to fund a training programme for single homeless people. It was launched in 2001 to mark the charity's 30th anniversary year.

Key to the strategy was forming a committee of influential business people who could contribute to the appeal and approach other businesses. 'Recruiting a chair for the appeal was another key factor, as this person would need to make a big personal commitment and become the public face of the appeal, asking for money in effect,' says Collins. It took around nine months to find the chair, Tommy Rodgers, managing director of transport and distribution firm, the TR Group.

Running high-profile fundraising events, including a gala ball for businesses, was another important strand of fundraising. This has now grown to six annual events as business contacts recruited for the big gift appeal have continued to support the charity.

Benefits

While employment benefits in the fundraising sector are often modest compared to those in the private sector, many organisations – particularly larger ones – are offering more attractive packages to lure skilled staff from other sectors. The Institute's 2004 survey shows that fundraisers enjoy a wide and eclectic range of benefits, from standard pension schemes to use of a company bicycle!

Pension schemes

Occupational pension schemes are the most widespread benefit, held by almost three quarters (73%) of fundraisers surveyed by the Institute.

If you are offered the chance to join a pension scheme as part of your remuneration package, it is likely to be a money purchase scheme. Research by Remuneration Economics shows that the vast majority (81%) of pension schemes in the voluntary sector are money purchase schemes; over 40% of those still offering final salary schemes (43%) reported that they were considering the viability of the scheme for new employees. This is due to the risks associated with such schemes, combined with relatively poor performance of equity markets in recent years.

And almost a third (31%) of charities offering money purchase schemes reported that they had previously operated a final purchase scheme, which was now closed to new employees (60% have closed them in the last two years).

Other benefits

Just over a third (33.5%) of fundraisers surveyed by the Institute receive a car or travel allowance and 10.3% have a health plan. Around 11% say they receive other benefits, such as:

- death in service benefit
- free entry to museums
- funding for professional development
- life insurance
- luncheon vouchers
- membership of Institute of Fundraising
- season ticket loan
- subsidised gym membership
- time off for volunteering

Regional variations

In terms of pensions, London fundraisers are best off with 79% getting a pension compared to fundraisers elsewhere in the south east, of whom only 56% list pensions among their benefits. However, funders in this region are more likely to have a company health plan (14%) than those based in London (9%) or Yorkshire and Humberside (5%).

Predictably perhaps fundraisers in London are least likely to be given a car or travel allowance: only 15% receive this benefit. However, in the north east some 53% of fundraisers enjoy these benefits as do 50% of fundraisers in the north west.

Fundraising focus: transferable skills

After 33 years in the RAF and at the age of 55, Squadron Leader John McNeil swapped his navigator seat in airborne early warning aircraft for a new career. He took with him skills including writing, an ability to get on with people and work in a team, self-discipline and an Open University maths-based BA.

He attended a career transition workshop – 'good, very interesting' – and read an article about charities in *Quest*, a magazine about retraining opportunities for people leaving the armed forces. He then went on a course run by Working for a Charity that provided 'an insight into working in the voluntary sector and a work placement'.

McNeil's subsequent job search led him to the British Red Cross, where he spent two years as senior fundraiser for Hertfordshire. 'I took over a going concern of programmes working with volunteers in the community, with a major event being the annual Flag Week in May,' he explains. He had 65 local organisers, each with their own team of volunteers.

Last year McNeil started a new job as Hertfordshire community fundraiser for Macmillan Cancer Relief. He has moved away from fixed events into a role coordinating more fluid activities and managing groups of volunteers: 'working twice as hard ... [as in the RAF] ... for much less money'.

With thanks to Questonline, www.questonline.co.uk

Working conditions

Charities and other fundraising organisations may not always be able to match the salaries available outside the sector. However, they often have the edge when it comes to flexible working practices and personal development opportunities. Many of these organisations now use work-life balance policies to attract and retain top quality professionals.

Working hours

Of the fundraisers surveyed by the Institute in 2004, 85% say they work full time; the remainder are employed on a part-time basis. Working hours vary from one organisation to another but most full-time, desk-based jobs will involve a minimum 35 hours a week. Additional hours may be required to attend evening meetings or weekend events; travel within a working day may be frequent and absence from home occasional if your job involves direct contact with sponsors, major donors or volunteers.

Work-life balance

Many fundraising organisations have introduced work-life balance policies to retain existing staff, attract skilled professionals looking for more flexible working arrangements and appeal to job returners.
    Work-life policies can include:

- compressed working hours
- job sharing
- flexi time
- part-time work
- time off in lieu (TOIL)
- unpaid sabbaticals
- working from home

As discussed in Section 2, it is possible to enter fundraising at any stage of your career and at any age. So it is common for a fundraiser to take a career break or work part-time or flexible hours to bring up a family or care for a relative. In fact flexible working is the main reason that 2.2% of fundraisers chose their current job while 2.7% say the chance to be self-employed was the key reason for choosing fundraising.

Job security

Several fundraising organisations – including a small number of household name charities – have made staff redundant in the past two

Personal perspective: Karen Boyle

Job: Special events manager

Organisation: British Lung Foundation (BLF)

Age: 28

Dealing with celebrities, including Ben Elton, Joanna Lumley and Caroline Ahearne for World Sight Day, was part of my role as publicity officer at Sight Savers in West Sussex. And when I moved to the Red Cross as events officer, I had great fun helping to organise the successful Desperate and Dateless Balls for single people aged 18–35, in 2002 and 2003. I also helped to organise a lecture by Nelson Mandela and a gala evening at the west end show *Bombay Dreams*, attended by the Queen.

The work can be glamorous but the downside is that the pay is worse than most other areas of fundraising. I have recently moved to the BLF where I plan to develop more challenge events. With 120 runners, the London Marathon is currently one of the biggest money-makers for the charity, along with an annual golf day, which attracts lots of celebrity support.

I'd recommend volunteering at charity events if considering this as a career. I volunteered at the Citizens Advice Bureau giving legal advice and representing people at tribunals while studying law at Glasgow University, and that was very helpful. I've worked in the voluntary sector since leaving university, first as events administrator for a small Scottish charity and then when I moved down to London – where there were more job opportunities – as an assistant for another small charity, Counsel and Care, before joining Sight Savers.

years. These decisions have been attributed to reasons such as falls in voluntary income and slumps in the investment markets.

The Institute's 2004 survey found that 82.7% of fundraisers had never been made redundant and a third (32.9%) have been working in fundraising for 11 years or more. More than a quarter (26.5%) – the biggest single group – have been fundraisers for between six and 10 years.

Diversity in fundraising

Workplace diversity means ensuring that a wide range of people are represented on the workforce and ensuring that factors such as age, disability, ethnicity and gender are not barriers to employment.

Charities and voluntary organisations have come under pressure in recent years to make their own workplaces as diverse as the groups they represent or work with. This pressure has been driven in part by an increase in these organisations delivering public services: income from statutory agencies now accounts for 37% of voluntary organisations' total income.

The London Development Agency (LDA) highlighted the need for charities to attract more black and minority ethnic (BME) fundraisers in its 2003 report, Reaching Multicultural Britain: the black and minority ethnic community and fundraising in the top charities.

The study of recruitment, retention and development of fundraisers from BME communities found that 70% did not have a member of the BME community at a senior level in fundraising. While 50% of the respondents said they were taking steps to recruit more employees from the BME communities, none used the BME press for job advertisements. The report recommended that charities should use the specialist press and BME professional networks to advertise job vacancies.

Sector Initiatives

The Institute of Fundraising has been working with the LDA, the Black Training and Enterprises Group (BTEG) and London Voluntary Services Council to train staff working in BME organisations as fundraisers to certificate level.

The National Council for Voluntary Organisations (NCVO) launched an initiative in 2001 to improve diversity in the voluntary sector. The work of the diversity project has included publications, events and training to encourage voluntary sector leaders and HR staff to consider diversity and incorporate it into their recruitment policies and practice.

In practical terms, this means that voluntary organisations are being encouraged to advertise their job vacancies – including those in fundraising – more widely, for example in specialist publications and through alternative formats.

Another initiative aimed at increasing diversity is the Museum Association's Diversify project. Launched in 1998, it is encouraging more museums and galleries to employ people from ethnic minority backgrounds through trainee schemes.

Diverse workforce

Women may face fewer employment barriers in fundraising than in other sectors. The Institute of Fundraising's 2004 membership survey shows that over two-thirds (68%) of fundraisers are women, which mirrors the 2002 UK Labour Force Survey figure for women in the wider voluntary sector workforce. The prevalence of flexible working, including part-time hours, may account for this in part.

The survey also highlights that age is unlikely to be a significant barrier to employment in fundraising. Just over a fifth of fundraisers are aged 45–54 and more than one in 10 are 55–64 years old.

Employers including those in the voluntary sector are currently under pressure from government and campaigning groups to employ more disabled people. The Disability Discrimination Act outlaws discrimination against a person on the grounds of their disability. Yet the Disability Rights Commission says one in eight young disabled people (13%) have been refused a job because of a reason related to their disability.

Employers displaying the Jobcentre Plus 'Positive about disabled people' logo (also known as the 'two ticks' logo) have agreed to meet five commitments regarding the recruitment, employment, retention and career development of disabled people. This includes offering an interview to all disabled applicants who meet the minimum criteria for a job vacancy and considering them on their abilities.

ⓘ *For further information contact the Commission for Racial Equality (www.cre.gov.uk), Disability Rights Commission (www.drc-gb.org) or Equal Opportunities Commission (www.eoc.org.uk)*

ⓘ *For information about NCVO's diversity project, visit www.ncvo-vol.org.uk*

ⓘ *For further details on the LDA research, visit www.lda.gov.uk*

ⓘ *See* **Directory** *for full contact details of organisations listed above*

Getting started

Introduction

Fundraisers come from a variety of backgrounds and often find that skills and experience gained in other sectors are useful and relevant to fundraising jobs. Increasingly sophisticated fundraising techniques and competition for funds means that the sector now offers entrants a long and varied career, with scope for professional development through formal and informal learning.

While formal fundraising qualifications have become more common in the sector, enthusiasm and related experience will also help to get you a foothold on the fundraising career ladder. The fundamental question that all prospective employers will want the answer to is: 'Can you raise money?' Having a fundraising qualification, a track record or related experience will show them that you can.

Where do fundraisers come from?

There is no single route into fundraising. Fundraisers may:

- join at junior level and work their way up
- move into fundraising from a related job (e.g. marketing or sales) in a different sector
- gain unpaid experience as a volunteer while in another job
- enter the sector via a graduate recruitment scheme or internship

The Institute of Fundraising's 2004 membership survey found that nearly half of respondents (48.8%) had worked in the private sector prior to moving into fundraising. The next most common routes into fundraising were from the public sector (16.4%) and education (15.9%). Only 8.2% had already worked in the voluntary sector.

And fundraisers are an eclectic bunch. While a number (1.8%) of survey respondents had previously worked with the army, navy or other forces, others came from arts marketing, broadcasting, journalism, law, secretarial, self-employment – and full-time parenting!

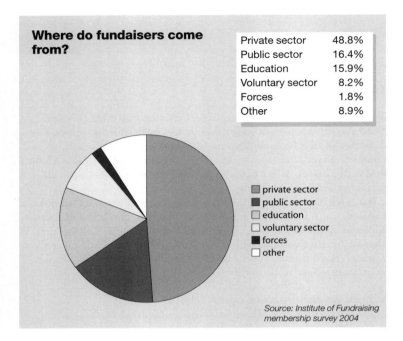

Where do fundaisers come from?

Private sector	48.8%
Public sector	16.4%
Education	15.9%
Voluntary sector	8.2%
Forces	1.8%
Other	8.9%

- private sector
- public sector
- education
- voluntary sector
- forces
- other

Source: Institute of Fundraising membership survey 2004

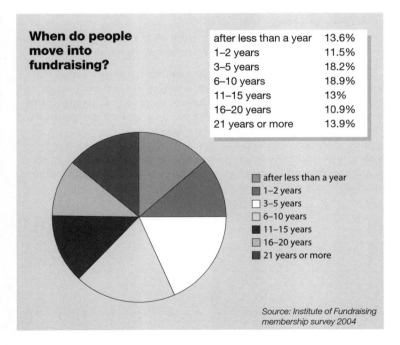

When do people move into fundraising?

after less than a year	13.6%
1–2 years	11.5%
3–5 years	18.2%
6–10 years	18.9%
11–15 years	13%
16–20 years	10.9%
21 years or more	13.9%

- after less than a year
- 1–2 years
- 3–5 years
- 6–10 years
- 11–15 years
- 16–20 years
- 21 years or more

Source: Institute of Fundraising membership survey 2004

Fundraising attracts people at every stage of their working career. The majority of fundraisers (62.2%) in the Institute survey had worked for 10 years or less before joining the sector. At the other end of the scale, a significant number (13.9%) had worked for 21 years or more before making their move. So it's never too early or too late to consider a job in this sector.

Pre-fundraising training

There are no hard and fast rules about the qualifications and training required to work in fundraising. Many people transfer the skills or experience they have gained in other sectors. Others pick up skills on the job or undertake training, particularly if they have chosen to specialise in a fundraising area such as legacies or corporate giving.

The Institute membership survey found that just under half (45.7%) of fundraisers have a degree. Around a fifth (21.6%) have undertaken professional training. However, a large number of respondents (43.4%) said they had been able to transfer skills they had acquired in previous jobs and so had not felt it necessary to do a training course before entering fundraising. Three quarters of those surveyed had done some sort of fundraising training since entering the sector. IT, marketing, staff management, legal issues and financial management are the most common areas of post-entry training.

Entry opportunities

Over half of fundraisers (58.1%) surveyed by the Institute said they had worked in a voluntary capacity before securing a paid position in the fundraising sector. Volunteering is an excellent way of learning about fundraising and can help you to decide what sort of organisation or role interests you.

As the Institute survey shows, most people come to fundraising after working in the private or public sectors. A small number join straight from university or college, going into starter positions such as fundraising assistant. Some may take part in a fundraising internship or placement or paid graduate training scheme. Although such schemes are less prevalent in the voluntary sector than the private sector, an increasing number of charities and other organisations are offering them. One in 10 respondents in the Institute survey said their organisation now offers a fundraising work placement.

Pre-entry qualifications, training and experience

General qualifications

Fundraising is still a relatively young industry and most successful fundraisers develop their skills through volunteering or learning on the job. Academic qualifications are less important than relevant skills or fundraising experience. Having said that, employers recruiting for even the most basic fundraising position will probably require you to have some or all of the following:

- GCSEs in English and maths
- one or more A or AS levels
- good computer and IT skills

Will having a degree help me get a job in fundraising?

There are currently no specific degree-level courses in fundraising. However, potential employers may consider a degree or similar qualification in business studies, management, marketing, media, public relations or sales as helpful. A qualification in one of these fields may also equip you with some of the skills needed for specialist fundraising roles, such as retail or events.

A degree-level qualification in marketing or a similar discipline may also be useful if you want to undertake postgraduate training in fundraising.

ⓘ *See* **Section 5 – Getting ahead** *for more information about fundraising training and professional development*

Graduate training schemes

In contrast to the commercial sector, there are very few graduate training schemes run by charities or other fundraising organisations. But if you can find one, the experience will provide a good kick-start to your voluntary or public sector career.

Ideally, graduate training schemes should offer you a structured programme of work experience supported by related training. Some

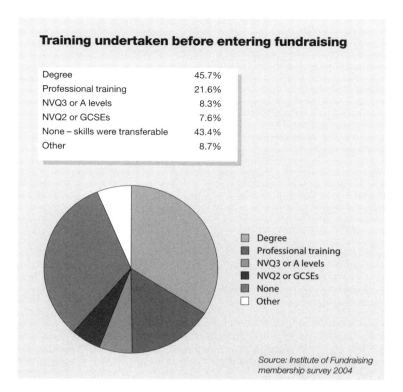

Training undertaken before entering fundraising

Degree	45.7%
Professional training	21.6%
NVQ3 or A levels	8.3%
NVQ2 or GCSEs	7.6%
None – skills were transferable	43.4%
Other	8.7%

Degree
Professional training
NVQ3 or A levels
NVQ2 or GCSEs
None
Other

Source: Institute of Fundraising
membership survey 2004

schemes also pair graduate trainees with a mentor who can offer advice and support the trainee's personal development.

As a trainee, you might be allocated a specific project to work on during your time with the organisation. You might also undertake a portion of your placement outside the fundraising team or department, perhaps in communications or research. Experience gained in different departments will give you a rounded view of the organisation and help you to understand how fundraising fits in.

In return for this experience, the fundraising organisation benefits from your skills. And having invested time and money to train you, the organisation will be keen to keep you on so that you can put your new skills to the test!

Your university or college careers service may have information about organisations currently running graduate training schemes. Information may also be available from graduate support organisations such as:

- Graduate Prospects (www.prospects.ac.uk) and for public/voluntary sector jobs, Getalife.org.uk (www.getalife.co.uk)

- the National Council for Work Experience (www.work-experience.org)
- the Ethical Careers Service (www.ethicalcareers.org)
- Doctorjob.com (www.doctorjob.com)

ⓘ> See Directory for full contact details and further resources

You could also approach fundraising organisations in your area of interest to find out if they run a graduate training scheme. If they don't, ask them whether they would consider organising one – and be prepared to persuade them of the benefits.

ⓘ> See Volunteering section (page 103) for tips on selling work placements to employers

ⓘ> See Section 1 for help with finding information about charities and other voluntary organisations

The following organisations have run training schemes for graduates in recent years:

Cancer Research UK (www.cancerresearchuk.org)

Offers a two-year graduate training scheme in fundraising and marketing, leading to a permanent role on successful completion. Each year, the scheme offers four to eight graduates paid experience in marketing, communications, development, strategy, national events, retail and community fundraising. Applicants are required to have at least a 2:1 honours degree (or equivalent) in any subject. They are also expected to demonstrate strategic thinking, excellent PC skills and be numerate and literate.

Trainees are based at the charity's offices in central London and undertake four six-month placements during their time there. In addition to specially designed training, graduates also take part in a mentoring programme. The starting salary for the scheme is around £20,000 per annum with the opportunity to join the charity's pension scheme. Information about the 2005 scheme is available from October 2004.

ⓘ> See Personal perspective, below

Charities Advisory Trust (www.charitiesadvisorytrust.co.uk)

A registered charity helping other charities to generate income through trading, the Charities Advisory Trust (CAT) offers two types of graduate training scheme. Its long-standing graduate internship is aimed at recent graduates and involves working on the charity's Card Aid Christmas card campaign, which raises over £1m for good causes through the sale of charity Christmas cards through temporary shops open between October and December each year.

Some interns may work at the trust's head office in London, coordinating the different aspects of running a Christmas card campaign and supporting the work of those in the shops. Interns may learn about fundraising administration, grant giving, volunteer management and initiatives such as CAT's Green Hotel in Mysore, India.

Most interns manage the trust's Card Aid shops. There are around 40 of these each year, based mainly in central London and also in Oxford, Cambridge, York and Leeds. Interns gain valuable experience of managing their own mini enterprise; responsibilities include stock control, volunteer management, customer service and public relations.

Internships vary in length but most begin in October (occasionally the office-based internships may begin in the summer and some shop internships not until November) and last at least until Christmas, with the possibility of extension within CAT to a permanent position (much of CAT's management is drawn from its previous interns). The internship salary is currently £13,250 pro rata.

CAT recently launched two advanced graduate internships for those who have had at least two years work experience after graduation (not necessarily in the voluntary sector). Interns work either on the Card Aid campaign or on the Good Gifts catalogue. Based in London, internships vary in length and finish at Christmas, although there is scope to move into a permanent position with the trust. The current salary for these posts is £17,250 pro rata.

All interns participate in a formal training programme, based around seminars on key aspects of the voluntary sector.

Christian Aid (www.christian-aid.org.uk)

The charity takes on a number of graduate interns each year, who are offered experience of various teams during their placement. Posts are advertised on the charity's website when they become available.

Examples from 2004 included an education internship based in the charity's schools and youth team. The internship is for an 11-month, fixed-term contract on a salary of £12,125 per annum. Activities include developing publications for schools.

Interns receive training in time and project management, internet publishing, gender and diversity awareness. Interns are allocated a mentor who helps them to develop a personal development plan.

NSPCC (www.nspcc.org.uk)

The National Society for the Prevention of Cruelty to Children (NSPCC) launched a graduate traineeship programme in 1986 but availability is subject to budgets. The last intake comprised two fundraising trainees who began their 12 month placement in autumn 2003. No traineeships are being offered in 2004 but the charity hopes to re-establish the programme in the future. Previous interns have secured permanent positions with the charity.

Oxfam (www.oxfam.org.uk)

Having run a successful graduate scheme for the last two years, Oxfam launched a voluntary graduate scheme in 2004. Most placements will last for four months (although the charity may consider slightly longer placements for applicants who are interested). The closing date for the 2004 intake was May 2004; placements were due to commence in September 2004. Recruitment for the 2005 scheme is from March 2005. Graduates are based in one of the charity's teams based in Oxford. These include fundraising, campaigns, communications and trading.

Oxfam says its aim is to match graduates with a department or project reflecting their area of interest. The scheme offers participants a range of experience, including:

- developing campaigns or links with donors
- building relationships with new sectors
- planning Oxfam events
- carrying out research

The scheme is open to those who are about to graduate, or who have graduated in the last two years with a 2:2 and who can demonstrate qualities such as creativity, professionalism and commitment to the work and values of Oxfam. Reasonable travel and lunch expenses are paid. Participants have a mentor and personal development opportunities during their placement. Oxfam hopes that trainees will secure ongoing employment with the charity at the end of the placement.

Royal Society for the Protection of Birds (www.rspb.org.uk)

In 2004, RSPB's graduate trainee programme included two full-time places as trainee fundraising and marketing officers. Based at the charity's headquarters in Bedfordshire, the programme offers trainees experience in regional and national fundraising, promoting RSPB's work and supporting membership recruitment.

Trainees should have a degree (or equivalent), be creative, possess business flair and a strong commitment to wildlife conservation. A two-year contract is offered, with a salary of around £15,000 per annum. The closing date for the 2004 programme was June 2004.

Other trainee schemes

Fundraising trainee programme

This programme run by Fundraising Training Ltd (www.frtr.co.uk) is designed to 'fast track' those committed to getting into fundraising, overcoming the two to three years experience that many fundraising positions require. The scheme is open to recent graduates and those with related work experience gained in areas such as marketing, sales or project management.

The scheme attracts up to 600 applications each year, from which around 30 are chosen for the six-month programme. Charities submit their trainee opportunities and candidates are short-listed for interview. Successful candidates undertake a training programme with Fundraising Training alongside their work. This comprises six one-day workshops spread over six months, covering statutory, trust and corporate fundraising. Trainees are allocated a personal tutor who provides two overall assessments during the training period. Trainees are also required to complete four work-based assignments which, if completed to a high enough standard, will give them module one of the Institute of Fundraising's Certificate in Fundraising Management.

Charities participate in the scheme to invest in fundraising for the first time, expand their fundraising team with a trainee post or find the right person if they have had difficulty filling a post. Charities pay the trainee's salary: £16,000–£18,000 for recent graduates; £18,000–£20,000 for those with up to five years of relevant experience; £20,000–£22,000 for those with over five years relevant experience.

Host organisations include 'household name' charities such as Age Concern, Salvation Army and Scope as well as smaller charities such as Pyramid Trust.

ProspectUs (www.prospect-us.co.uk) is a recruitment agency specialising in not-for-profit jobs in London. It has in the past promoted this trainee programme.

Personal perspective: Claire Huston

Job: Fundraising and marketing graduate trainee

Organisation: Cancer Research UK

Age: 22

I was in the first intake of graduate trainees following the merger of the Imperial Cancer Research Fund and the Cancer Research Campaign in 2002. I found out about the scheme in 2002 at an alternative careers fair that I went to in my first year at university. ICRF had a stand there and I was interested so kept the brochure for the next two years!

My degree was in English language and literature but I'd also done voluntary work at university, been a production manager for a play and treasurer for a society. So I could demonstrate that I'd worked on projects and had good time management skills – some of the things the charity looks for in trainees. I really wanted to work in a job where I was making a difference.

What appealed to me about the Cancer Research UK scheme was that you could get really wide experience from the four placements you did over two years, which helps with career progression. And one of the best things is that you're really needed – they're not just creating a post for you. The starting salary of £20,000 including London weighting seems competitive – somewhere in the middle of graduate schemes in the City and first jobs in PR.

My first six-month placement was in legacy marketing where I was involved in two mailings – one to solicitor contacts and a cold mailing to the public. It was a really interesting place to start. You learn all about direct marketing, pick up the jargon and get experience of dealing with designers and printers.

My next placement was in community fundraising. Initially my job was to co-ordinate the breast cancer awareness campaign, which involved overseeing posters, leaflets and the website. Then I requested some 'real' community fundraising experience so went to shadow a community fundraiser working near Gatwick. I ended up covering for her for two weeks while she was on holiday and attended events such as a company barbecue to receive money raised for the charity. It was good to see what supporters are doing to raise money and witness first hand their enthusiasm for the cause.

After that, I moved to the development department where I worked with the other graduate trainees on the All Clear awareness campaign. This time, the focus was on internal communication to staff and working on the launch event.

I'm now on my final placement and have moved out of the fundraising and marketing department and into clinical, corporate and external affairs to work on the SunSmart skin cancer awareness campaign. This includes dealing with quite complex queries and also co-ordinating Popwatch, which involves the SunSmart team attending Party in the Park events during the summer.

As part of the scheme, I have a mentor who I have a meeting with once a month to check that my personal development is progressing. As well as the experience on each placement, trainees get general training in areas like presentation skills and time management. Switching jobs every six months means it's a steep learning curve but at the end of it, you're able to demonstrate that you're incredibly adaptable.

At the end of the placement, trainees put together a mini CV with their strengths, areas of development and type of role they're interested in. These go forward to the directors of fundraising and marketing, who look at where we could fit in. Given the amount of time they've invested in you, they try to hold on to you and find a position where you will feel happy and challenged.

Volunteering

Volunteering is an excellent way to gain relevant experience while also showing a genuine commitment to the voluntary sector. The Institute of Fundraising's 2004 membership survey found that 58.1% of fundraisers had worked in a voluntary capacity before securing a paid position in the sector.

Most consultants advise that you volunteer in a fundraising department to get direct experience. This should also help you to decide on your preferred area of fundraising, ready for serious job hunting. What's more, it will provide a prime opportunity for networking with people already working as fundraisers.

Most charities welcome enthusiastic volunteers and many advertise opportunities on their websites. Some larger charities have volunteer co-ordinators, while others deal with volunteers through their personnel departments. Otherwise, contact the head of fundraising directly to talk about volunteering. Offering your services should be beneficial for both you and the organisation, so be very clear about what you are aiming to get out of the exercise when you approach them.

Remember to conduct yourself professionally at all times while volunteering – the experience could turn out to be an extended interview if a post becomes available at the organisation.

Volunteering opportunities

There are numerous opportunities for you to do voluntary work in a fundraising environment. Make a list of the organisations or type of organisation (e.g. environment charity, theatre etc) you'd like to work for. Then make a list of the skills you can offer them (e.g. research or IT) and the experience that you're looking for (e.g. events management or community fundraising). This should help you to narrow down the list to those organisations most likely to benefit from your volunteering.

The range of organisations and opportunities include:

- Charities and voluntary organisations: researching a new service or project; designing a new website; helping to run a shop or other commercial activity; becoming a charity trustee
- Arts/heritage organisations: identifying grantmaking bodies; working with corporate supporters on sponsored events
- Universities: researching potential donors from alumni
- Hospitals: working with local media to secure coverage of fundraising events
- Political organisations/think tanks/trade unions: researching donations and sponsorship to fund project work

If you're still studying, get involved with your university or college rag committee or any other student volunteering programmes. Most recruiters say they expect to see evidence of voluntary experience gained as a student when placing graduates in their first role, usually as a fundraising administrator or co-ordinator.

Many voluntary organisations work with universities and colleges to advertise their volunteering opportunities – including fundraising jobs – to students. Your university or college may also have a matching service, where you can register your interest in fundraising and be matched with an organisation looking for help in this area.

Some fundraising organisations may be willing to offer you a voluntary work placement during your holidays. This could involve working on a specific project such as a new fundraising campaign or donor research. Your careers service may have details of organisations that offer such placements. Other resources include the National Council for Work Experience (NCWE), whose website (www.work-experience.org.uk) lists vacation placements and internships.

If you can't find what you're looking for, ask the organisation that you're interested in working for whether they would consider offering you a voluntary work placement. Be prepared to sell your skills and to explain what you can offer them. The NCWE offers useful advice and information on the benefits to both employers and students of work placements (see below).

Selling work experience to an employer

A student can help you:
- be more profitable
- reduce costs
- make better use of time

A student can help develop your business by bringing:
- new ideas and fresh enthusiasm
- an extra resource
- additional skills to tackle projects otherwise put on the backburner
- IT skills and knowledge of new technologies
- a cost effective and flexible solution to your recruitment needs

Today's university students:
- can focus on business issues and solutions
- resolve business problems effectively
- are good team workers
- can think for themselves and get on with it

Typical projects undertaken by students include:
- marketing and market research
- developing IT systems
- design and implementation of databases
- creating a website
- research and development
- writing new software
- reviewing work processes and efficiency

Source: National Council for Work Experience

Finding a volunteering position

Many organisations list their volunteering opportunities on their website. Some also advertise them in their own newsletters or supporter magazines. Other places to look for vacancies include:

- your local library or community centre
- local newspapers
- your local volunteer bureau (find at www.volunteering.org.uk)
- recruitment agencies and job websites
- The Guardian's Society supplement on Wednesday and for volunteering information, society.guardian.co.uk/volunteering
- The Evening Standard's Just the Job supplement on Monday
- The Big Issue
- National Volunteering Database (www.do-it.org.uk)

- Timebank (www.timebank.org.uk)
- Community Service Volunteers (www.csv.org.uk)
- OneWorld (www.oneworld.org)
- Reach (www.volwork.org.uk)
- Common Purpose/Just do something (www.citizensconnection.net)
- Student Volunteering England (www.studentvol.org.uk)

ⓘ *See* **Directory** *for full contact details and more resources*

Organisations that have offered fundraising work placements in recent years include:

Action for Blind People (www.afbp.org)

The London-based charity offers a 12-month voluntary position in the fundraising team, which it says is ideal for undergraduates on a sandwich degree course.

The trainee gains experience in a wide range of fundraising techniques including events, community, major donors and new developments. Specific tasks include researching new activities and supporting the fundraising team on major projects. The trainee is also given responsibility for a number of projects of their own. Applicants are expected to be computer literate and able to work well in a team. Reasonable travel expenses will be reimbursed. Hours are negotiable.

CSV (www.csv.org.uk)

Community Service Volunteers is the UK's largest volunteering organisation, placing over 128,000 volunteers each year. CSV works with partner organisations to fill vacancies in areas including media, environment and education. There are specific programmes for young people and retired professionals as well as opportunities for employee volunteering and weekend volunteering. CSV also runs the annual Make a Difference Day volunteering event.

The Experience Corps (www.experiencecorps.co.uk)

An independent, non-profit-making company set up with funding from the Home Office to encourage people aged 50 and over to offer their skills and experience in their local communities. The organisation has a team of 'animators' based in every region of England who match volunteers to organisations in the public and voluntary sectors.

The Prince's Trust (www.princes-trust.org.uk)

Founded in 1976 by The Prince of Wales to help young people fulfil their potential, the trust offers a range of opportunities including training, personal development, business start up support, mentoring and advice. Volunteers can work in several capacities such as fundraisers, mentors for young businesses or for those leaving care, and assessors of community projects.

The World Land Trust (www.worldlandtrust.org)

This conservation charity offers six-month internships based at its offices in Suffolk. Interns are assigned work on one of the charity's overseas conservation management projects. This gives them hands-on experience of project management, fundraising and general office/administrative skills. Interns also get an individually tailored training programme to suit their needs.

Internships are entirely voluntary, although work-related expenses such as travel to meetings and training courses are reimbursed. Previous interns have found employment in conservation or related areas.

REACH (www.volwork.org.uk)

Reach matches people with managerial, professional, business and technical experience with part-time voluntary roles at UK organisations, from large national charities to small grass-roots community groups. It has around 3,000 volunteering opportunities on its database and places more than 1,000 volunteers each year. Volunteers use their skills and experience to support a specific project; previous examples include devising a fundraising lottery, setting up income-generating community enterprises and marketing services to new audiences.

Introductory courses

If you want to get an idea of what it is like to work in the voluntary sector or in fundraising before applying for a job then a 'taster' course may be helpful. These courses provide a useful introduction both to the voluntary sector and to fundraising itself. As well as fundraising, these courses often cover working with volunteers, general sector trends and job hunting techniques.

The following organisations run introductory courses:

Working for a Charity (www.wfac.org.uk)

Offers courses for people looking for their first voluntary sector job. Prices range from £60 for the introductory programme to £595 for the intensive programme. Courses include:

- Introductory programme: takes place over two evenings – one of which looks at fundraising – and is intended to provide an overview of the charity sector. The course is suitable for those wanting a brief introduction to the sector and information on job opportunities.
- Foundation course: aimed at those seeking a new career in the voluntary sector, or wishing to return to work, including those considering part-time or flexible employment options. The course combines seven days of seminars, including sessions on fundraising,

marketing, funding sources and job opportunities. Trainees also undertake a 21-day voluntary work placement in a host charity. The course can be completed within a period of 8–12 weeks, with an average commitment of two to three days each week.

- Intensive programme: three-day course designed to meet the needs of people in full-time employment who wish to explore opportunities in the voluntary sector with minimal disruption to their current job. Includes sessions on fundraising and income generation.

Fresh Fields Training (01373 472469)

Provides training for people who want to work in the voluntary sector. Runs a two-day weekend residential course covering sector history and trends, fundraising methods and job-hunting advice. Price £225 including accommodation (concessions available for students and unemployed people). Also offers interview coaching sessions for individuals, from £50–£75 per session.

Institute of fundraising (www.institute-of-fundraising.org.uk)

The Institute runs an introduction to fundraising accredited training programme for those who are new to fundraising or for whom fundraising is a small part of their role including volunteers, trustees and service deliverers. The five-session programme covers the role of fundraising and the fundraiser, the planning cycle, techniques, regulation and ethics.

The Fundraising Programme (www.dsc.org.uk/charitytraining)

Run by the Institute of Fundraising and the Directory of Social Change, the programme offers a range of training from courses for the novice fundraiser to advanced courses that lead to the Institute's Certificate in Fundraising Management. The programme covers four levels of training, with the introductory level aimed at those who are new to fundraising or to a particular area of fundraising. Courses at this level include an overview of effective fundraising and 'how to' courses on raising money from trusts, companies, legacies, statutory sources and major donors.

ⓘ› *See* **Directory** *for full contact details*

ⓘ› *See* **Section 5: Getting ahead** *for more about training*

Switching sectors

The shortage of experienced fundraisers in the voluntary sector and the ongoing need to boost donations means that more and more organisations are looking at candidates from the commercial and public sectors. These candidates can offer a range of transferable skills and proven business experience, which fundraising organisations are finding essential in an increasingly competitive marketplace.

Many recruitment consultants working in the not-for-profit sector say that corporate candidates perceive 'charity' jobs as being much easier than 'real' jobs. Yet fundraising organisations face the same challenges as their commercial counterparts, whether this is retaining their donors (the customers) or developing their services (the products). A firm grasp of what's happening in the sector and a realistic vision of how you can contribute to its success will help your job-hunting enormously.

Getting started

Research is the key to switching sectors. First – and perhaps most importantly – you need to carry out extensive research to find out if a career in the voluntary sector is right for you. What opportunities exist for you to use your skills and experience? Which type or area of fundraising are you most interested in? Does the sector offer the type of career progression that you are looking for? And will a job in fundraising meet your salary expectations?

Before you start looking for a job, it might be helpful to conduct a personal 'skills audit' where you write down your key skills and then think about how you could use them in a fundraising role. For example, experience of account handling or business development may make you ideally suited to a job in corporate fundraising, where you are expected to nurture business relationships. If you have good research or presentation skills, a job in trust or lottery fundraising may be the perfect choice.

❶▸ *See* **Research** *section (below) for further information*

Volunteering or secondments are a good way of gaining experience if you are still working in the corporate sector but thinking of switching to fundraising. Many companies now have employment volunteering programmes or support particular charities. Find out which charities your organisation has links with and get involved in your spare time, if there isn't a formal secondment programme.

After leaving school, I worked for an agricultural company for 22 years. But I was made redundant at the age of 38, when the company was bought out.

By chance, I saw a story in the local paper about a volunteer who was about to retire after raising £150,000 to build a local hospice. I approached the charity and offered my services as a fundraiser for a six-month trial and stayed for 10 years, during which time the hospice was built and I became the hospice's first fundraising manager.

While still passionate about the hospice, I felt after this period that it was time to move on and spent several years in the leisure industry, including seven years at the Ayr United Football Club. When I saw an advert for fundraising manager at the Ayrshire Hospice, I decided to apply, as I loved my time there.

Despite my fears that they would be looking for someone younger, I got the job. And now I have a target of £3.5 m, as opposed to the £600,000 when I started there in 1986. Common sense, enthusiasm, people skills and a good understanding of the local area and media are all vital for this role.

What help is available?

There are an enormous number of useful resources available to career switchers, from websites to specialist training courses. Once you've decided that you want to work in fundraising, you could:

- register your details with a recruitment agency or online recruitment service
- have an informal chat with a recruitment consultant or experienced fundraiser to find out where your skills and experience can be best used
- keep an eye on the 'trade' publications and online resources to keep up-to-date with fundraising news and job opportunities
- contact organisations that you are interested in working for to find out about vacancies (their websites often list the latest ones)
- sign up for a course that offers an introduction to the voluntary sector and/or fundraising (see **Introductory courses**, above)
- attend sector events to find out about the latest fundraising issues and challenges

ⓘ *See **Directory** for details of recruitment resources, fundraising publications and websites, training courses and sector events*

Personal perspective: Joan Carrier

Job: Shop manager

Organisation: Roy Castle Lung Cancer Foundation

Age: 53

I've worked in retail all my life, starting as a window dresser and eventually becoming an area supervisor for 26 shops. When I returned to work after having a family, I wanted to use my skills to give something back to the community. I lost my mother when she had a heart attack due to smoking-related illness and this charity carries out lots of research and provides a counselling service for smokers who want to give up. Plus it's a small charity, so you can have lots of personal impact.

My background in commercial retail has helped a lot, as charity shops have to be run like ordinary stores nowadays. The rent is high and we only get a small discount for the rates. Display is very important too, as people prefer to donate their things to shops that look nice, as well as buy from them.

People management is another key skill required for this role, as there are around 25 volunteers who work at the shop each week. Most of them are older people who have retired but don't want to just 'veg' out, although we do get younger people who want work experience too. And I organise lots of social activities, usually nights out or garden parties, to thank them for their time.

Transferring your skills

Many charities see recruitment as a risky exercise and as fundraising often provides the lifeblood of the whole organisation, recruiting new fundraisers can be seen as an even higher risk. So it's your job to take the risk factor out of the equation by demonstrating just what a safe bet you will be. And if you don't already have a track record in fundraising, proving that you have transferable skills will be vital.

First, you need to identify the skills you have already gained from all areas of your life (not just paid work) and ascertain any that you need to learn. Look at job adverts, then send off for application packs to research the types of skills required for different fundraising jobs. They should be spelled out in detail in the person specification, which accompanies the job description and application form.

Think about your experience:

- in related disciplines e.g. marketing, public relations
- of similar roles e.g. telesales for donor recruitment, research for trust fundraising

- of working as a volunteer
- of working with volunteers

Consider any previous experience in areas such as:

- administration
- communications
- finance
- human resources
- IT
- marketing
- office management
- public relations
- sales

Recruitment consultants should be able to offer further advice on how to highlight your skills and experience. Tips are often included in 'introduction to fundraising' courses: Working for a Charity's foundation course includes a session with an HR consultant on this topic.

Five steps to help find your transferable skills

- Choose five skills that you have (and that you value)
- Think of specific examples where you have used each of these skills (these may be work or home related)
- Think about the skills you might need to do the job you want
- Have you got them?
- If not, how are you going to develop them?

Source: Working for a Charity

So demonstrating transferable skills will be the key to getting a job if you do not have direct experience in a similar role in the voluntary job. It shows your understanding of the role and that you are a low-risk option.

Skills for the job

Here are some examples of the top transferable skills for different areas of fundraising:

Corporate

Business development and/or account management from a number of commercial areas including public relations, advertising, marketing and service provision. Brand management, particularly within the pharmaceutical and food industries.

Events

It's a straightforward transfer from organising events for the commercial sector to organising them in the voluntary sector.

Trusts

Research and writing skills are key for trust roles.

Direct marketing/legacy fundraising

Like-for-like transfer from a direct marketing role in the commercial sector to a similar role in the voluntary sector.

Community

Relationship skills are key. A sales background is useful or, for a first jobber, rag experience gained at university.

Major donors

High-level face-to-face selling and relationship-building skills.

Source: Kage Partnership

Personal perspective: Hilary Hares

Job: Director of fundraising

Organisation: Treloar Trust

Age: 52

I spent 33 years in the commercial world before moving to the charity sector. Originally I trained as a shorthand typist and ended up working in human resources. In 1980, I was working as a personnel manager at a medium-sized London company when I saw an advert for a job managing the Allied Dunbar Foundation [now the Zurich Advice Network Foundation]. I hadn't raised a farthing before but I got the job. I did a three-day Institute of Fundraising course and the rest was learned on the job.

As a grantmaker, you have to speak the language of business while understanding the voluntary sector. My previous experience and understanding of sales and marketing were useful for this. I spent 14 years as manager of the foundation, after which I went on a three-year secondment to Business in the Community as development director of the Cares InCorporated employee volunteering programme. Here the challenge was bringing together business, the voluntary sector, local government and other key community stakeholders.

I took seven months off when I broke my leg and decided that I had learned a lot about fundraising and volunteering but wanted to be more involved with the beneficiaries. There is such great value in knowing who you are raising money for. In 2001 I joined The Treloar Trust, which provides education and other opportunities for young people with disabilities. My task as director of fundraising is to raise around £2m a year. We've succeeded in meeting our targets by moving from one off grants to two- and three-year funding packages and ongoing gifts.

The big mistake people make when they want to move into fundraising is not flagging up their transferable skills, such as sales or marketing knowledge. CVs need to reflect this as charities are looking for multi-skilled people with varied experience.

People often believe that working for a charity is a 'soft option' but that's not the case. I actually think it is more difficult than working in the commercial sector because companies don't start with an empty bank account at the start of each year!

My early career was varied to say the least – I was a nursing assistant, a harbour officer for customs and immigration, a lifeboatman and a Royal Air Force engineer. I volunteered for charities and completed a degree in social science and policy while still serving for the RAF. In fact, I had part-time, paid telephone fundraising work for the two years before I completed my service as part of my exit programme.

Joining Wildlife Network as fundraising officer was my first full-time fundraising role and the charity was small enough to allow me to try a number of initiatives across a range of disciplines, including trusts, corporate, community events and major donors. My first task there was to guide the organisation to charitable status and develop its fundraising strategy.

At the same time, I volunteered as a trustee for a small charity, Children Today, when it was set up in 1996 and became chair two years later. There, I worked with the chief executive, mainly on fundraising programmes and advising on how to distribute grants to the disabled children and families who formed the client group.

I found that I was enjoying detailed fundraising applications most, so took a post as RNIB lottery fundraising officer in 1998. Lottery applications require very detailed and structured information about the project, services and needs of the clients, to show what the work is all about. I enjoy being closely involved with the service delivery, or 'front-end' of the charity's mission and strategy.

I was promoted to senior lottery fundraising officer in 2000 and have had training in management, disability equality, media and controlling budgets to help equip me for the role. And getting close to what's going on, by meeting the people using and delivering services to the more than two million people in the UK with sight problems, is what continues to motivate me.

Research

You spend a large part of your life at work, so doing a job you love is important both for you and for the organisation that you join. The more information you can gather to help inform your decision, the better. It will stand you in good stead for applications and interviews, when your potential employer will call upon you to explain your reasons for wishing to pursue a career in the voluntary sector.

By now, you should have decided on why you want to work in fundraising and which sectors or roles interest you (see Section 2: Jobs in fundraising). You should also have identified the skills you need and those you already have. The next step is to find out more about the organisations and jobs available.

It's your job to impress potential employers by demonstrating your commitment and understanding of the sector. But you do need to be aware of the cultural differences – lack of resources, decision-making by committee and responsibility to a wide range of stakeholders – to help you decide if it is the right environment for you to work in. There may well be a drop in salary too – another important consideration for potential sector switchers.

Five steps to a career in fundraising

The following five-point plan should help you to start your job hunting research. More detailed information about volunteering and advice on applications can be found elsewhere in this section.

ⓘ *See* **Directory** *for details of relevant websites, publications, recruitment consultants, events and training courses*

Step 1. Research the wider sector

Who do you want to raise money for? You may have already decided that you want to work for a particular charity or cause. Alternatively, you might be interested in fundraising but unsure about which sector (e.g. arts, education) you would like to work in. Some basic knowledge of the developments and trends affecting fundraising organisations will help you to decide which sector is best for you.

Check out relevant websites for news and information about who might be recruiting. The Guardian's Society supplement and

SocietyGuardian website are a good starting point for voluntary and public sector news.

If you're looking for information about a specific sector, investigate websites maintained by the relevant umbrella organisation or trade body e.g. the National Council for Voluntary Organisations for charities or the Museums Association for museums.

Trade publications (see Directory) are another source of information about fundraising trends and future developments.

Step 2. Identify your ideal fundraising role

Are you interested in raising funds for a local organisation or would a large, national organisation be more appealing? Do you want to work with corporate donors or would you prefer a job that involved contact with individual donors? Find out more about the different methods of fundraising (see Section 1) and the fundraising roles available (see Section 2).

For further information about roles in fundraising, visit the Institute of Fundraising's website. The Voluntary Sector National Training Organisation (VSNTO) has produced a guide to fundraising national occupational standards, which examines the specific skills involved in different fundraising roles at different levels (see Section 5).

Assess where your skills lie and whether you need more training. Have you gained skills or experience that may be useful for a fundraising post? Or do you need to do a stint of voluntary work or a fundraising training course to make yourself more marketable?

Step 3. Consult specialist recruitment agencies and websites

Spend some time checking out the sites of recruitment agencies specialising in fundraising, as many provide useful tips for getting into the industry. Many list current vacancies so you can get an idea of which fundraising roles are most in demand and what level of salary they command.

Once you've carried out some initial research, call recruitment agencies and ask for a chat with the consultant specialising in fundraising. Some agencies offer careers counselling services specifically aimed at career switchers.

Step 4. Make contact with your target organisations

Use a resource such as NCVO's Voluntary Agencies Directory to find out more about organisations in which you are interested. Then check out their website if they have one: as well as providing news about their activities, vacancies are often advertised under a 'Jobs' or 'Careers' section.

You might also want to speak to someone at the organisation that you are interested in working for. One recruitment consultant says that fundraising directors and managers are usually pleased to make time to speak to people who are interested in their work. A word of warning though: there is no such thing as a totally informal chat or meeting. Think of these people as potential employers and make sure that you conduct yourself well at all times. Show interest, enthusiasm and be polite – you may find yourself being interviewed by them one day!

Step 5. Get some experience of the sector

Do some voluntary work – it will give you valuable first-hand experience of working in the fundraising sector or discipline in which you are interested. And attend local fundraising events to see fundraisers in action. See Volunteering section (above) for more information.

Meeting and talking to people already working in the voluntary sector is another good way to gather information. And many organisations – particularly smaller ones with a limited budget for recruitment advertising – rely on word of mouth to attract fundraisers.

Attending charity recruitment fairs or exhibitions can provide excellent networking opportunities; these events sometimes offer seminars or workshops too.

The Guardian and Guardian Unlimited

The Guardian

The Guardian provides coverage of fundraising, the sectors in which fundraisers work and job opportunities, through the following weekly supplements:

- **Media:** Provides latest news, gossip and jobs in the media sector, including coverage of marketing, fundraising and new media. (Monday)
- **Society:** Provides news, analysis, comment and jobs for people working in public services and the voluntary sector. Covers charities and voluntary organisations, health, housing, local government, regeneration and social care. (Wednesday)
- **Education:** Offers a combination of news, resources and jobs to academic professionals, teachers and students in higher, further and secondary education. (Tuesday)

Guardian Unlimited

Guardian Unlimited (www.guardian.co.uk) combines the editorial excellence of the Guardian and the Observer with the depth, immediacy and interactivity of the net. It is the UK's most popular website, with more users than any other UK newspaper on the net. The network includes a news service, extensive archive search facility, special reports and interactive guides.

The following sites are part of the Guardian Unlimited network:

- MediaGuardian.co.uk (media.guardian.co.uk)
- SocietyGuardian.co.uk (society.guardian.co.uk)
- EducationGuardian.co.uk (education.guardian.co.uk)

Politics (guardian.co.uk/politics)

This spin-off from the news site includes news, comment and analysis of UK politics and a comprehensive politics database, Ask Aristotle. Also includes special reports on key areas such as politics and the media plus information on political party funding and think tanks.

Guardian Unlimited Jobs (jobs.guardian.co.uk)

Here you will find a searchable database of all the vacancies advertised in the weekly supplements. Also includes careers advice and links to recruitment agencies.

Jobmatch for Fundraisers (jobs.guardian.co.uk/jobmatch)

The Guardian also offers a fundraising 'Jobmatch' service, designed to match fundraisers and would-be fundraisers with those who need their skills. Jobhunters can register their details with the service and receive email alerts as soon as vacancies that match their skills appear on the database. The service also enables employers to send vacancy information directly to people who meet their vacancy profile.

ⓘ▶ *See* Section 5 *for more information about Jobmatch*

Personal perspective: Gill Astarita

Job: Chief executive

Organisation: Volunteer Reading Help

As director of development at Action for Blind People (ABP), I managed an 80-strong team of staff in the fundraising, marketing, public affairs and information service departments. Between 1999 and 2004 I helped the charity to increase its voluntary income from £4m to over £14m. I achieved this by restructuring the fundraising team and winning the backing of the trustees for a major investment in fundraising.

Fundraising wasn't my first choice of career though. I graduated in 1988 with a first class honours degree in social sciences and wanted to pursue a career in academic research. I hadn't even considered working for a charity but getting a temporary fundraising assistant post at War on Want changed all that. I liked the culture and atmosphere and the fact that I was doing something for a great cause, so I applied for a permanent post there.

My next job was fundraising manager at Prisoners Abroad and after a year I was promoted to deputy director at the age of 28. Fundraising for such an unpopular cause was a real challenge – we focused on cases where people were likely to be more sympathetic to raise money.

Addaction, where I moved next to set up a fundraising and PR team from scratch, was another tough cause to raise funds for. At the time, people thought drug users and alcoholics had 'brought it on themselves' and would ask why they should help. But I always picked causes that I was passionate about and that made a big difference.

My advice, especially to other women as many still tend to be self-effacing, is to go for it – apply for the top jobs. After all, what's the worst that can happen?

Job hunting and application advice

Where to look for jobs

There is a growing number of places where fundraising vacancies are advertised, from the trade press and specialist websites to supporter magazines and mailings by umbrella organisations.

ⓘ *See* **Directory** *section for full details of the organisations mentioned below and other resources*

Recruitment consultants

There are several specialist recruitment agencies that can help you find a fundraising position in the charity sector, education, health and the arts.
Recruitment agencies will normally want to know:

- what type of work you are seeking
- which fundraising sector (e.g. charities, arts) you want to work in
- your salary expectations
- the geographical area in which you wish to work
- yours skills and experience, gained either in a paid or voluntary capacity

You should also consider contacting less specialised recruitment agencies, as some organisations will use their local agencies to recruit staff.

ⓘ *See* **Directory** *for full details and further resources*

Specialist press

Most organisations advertise their vacancies in newspapers and magazines that offer specialist coverage of fundraising and related areas.
Specialist press with **general fundraising** jobs include:

- The Guardian's Media supplement
- The Times's Public Agenda supplement
- Professional Fundraising
- Precision Marketing
- Marketing Week

For fundraising jobs in **charities and voluntary organisations**, the 'trade' magazines include:

- Charity Times
- Charity Finance
- Regeneration & Renewal
- Third Sector
- Voluntary Sector

Specialist publications with jobs in **arts fundraising** include:

- Arts Professional
- Museums Journal

Some organisations may place their jobs adverts in publications aimed at a particular target group, such as the black and minority ethnic (BME) community. These publications include:

- Asian Times
- Caribbean Times
- Eastern Eye
- Jewish Chronicle
- The Voice

The Commission for Racial Equality (www.cre.gov.uk) maintains an extensive list of ethnic minority publications.

ⓘ▷ *See* **Directory** *for full contact details and further resources*

Recruitment websites

The number of recruitment websites has mushroomed in recent years and there are now numerous online resources for anyone looking for a job in fundraising. Typically, these allow jobseekers to search a jobs database and sign up for vacancy alerts by email. Fundraising organisations and recruitment agencies pay to advertise their jobs; ads for voluntary posts are usually free.

Recruitment websites with fundraising jobs include:

- www.charityjobs.com
- www.charitycareers.co.uk
- www.fundraising.co.uk
- www.getalife.org.uk
- www.jobs.guardian.co.uk
- www.jobsincharities.co.uk

ⓘ▷ *See* **Directory** *for full contact details and further resources*

Careers fairs and recruitment events

Many colleges and universities organise 'alternative' careers fairs, where charities and other fundraising organisations take a stand to promote their activities. Although these organisations may not have jobs on offer, these events are a good opportunity to find out more about their fundraising activities. You might also want to inquire about volunteering opportunities.

Graduate Prospects (www.prospects.ac.uk) maintains an extensive list of graduate and postgraduate fairs in the UK, including those attracting voluntary and public sector employers. One of the largest events is Kaleidoscope (www.graduatecareersonline.com/fairs/kaleidoscope), a careers information fair run by the University of Manchester and UMIST Careers Service. Exhibitors at the 2004 Kaleidoscope fair included Barnardo's, The Big Issue in the North, The Lowry, People's History Museum, United Response and Victim Support.

Forum3 (www.forum3.co.uk) is an annual recruitment and volunteering fair for the not-for-profit sector. In addition to exhibitors from the voluntary sector, there are sessions on fundraising, personal development and volunteering. The 2004 event, held in October, includes a new 'fundraising zone' for visitors looking to enter fundraising or further develop their career in the sector. Advice and information is provided by the Institute of Fundraising, Directory of Social Change and Forum3 organiser Charity People.

Sector events

There are a number of professional development events for charities and other fundraising organisations. You may find it useful to attend one or more of these as part of your job hunting: as well as covering fundraising, these events provide a good introduction to other issues in the voluntary sector such as finance, IT and volunteering.

Events include:

- Institute of Fundraising National Convention (www.institute-of-fundraising.org.uk)
  Annual three-day learning and networking event for fundraisers. Offers plenaries, workshops and sessions for all levels of experience. A Careerbank feature was introduced for 2004, offering specialist advice to fundraisers on personal and career development.
- Charityfair (www.dsc.org.uk/charityfair)
  Annual two-day learning and skills event organised by the Directory of Social Change. Provides workshops, masterclasses and introductory sessions on a range of voluntary sector issues including fundraising.

ⓘ *See* **Directory** *at the back of this guide for full details and other sector events*

Personal perspective: Corporate fundraiser

Following Forum3 in 2002, I found a full-time paid job with a care charity as corporate fundraiser.

I attended two seminars that convinced me I was right to want a change of career and sector. The presentations helped me realise that I had the necessary skills to operate successfully in the sector and bring something of value to a charity. The opportunity to meet various people was also of great value.

My previous role was as a relationship manager at an investment bank, maintaining existing account relationships and selling multi-currency account products to prospective clients in the non-bank financial institutions sector (i.e. to fund managers and insurance companies).

After deciding to move into the charity sector it became increasingly clear to me that my sales and relationship management experience and skills in banking were closely allied to those needed to be a successful fundraiser. Where I was segmenting the market and researching potential customers, you need the same type of skill to identify potential donors; for existing customers, read existing supporters; for implementing new business, read launching a new partnership; for customer service, read maintaining the donor base; and so on.

The most time-consuming part of the process was changing my CV to strip it of jargon, to make it understandable to an entirely different audience, and make it clear that my skills were transferable. I lost count of how many versions of my CV I wrote.

The most challenging part of the process was convincing people of my motivations for making the transition, and why it was viable for me to drop from being a high earner at an investment bank to the relatively low pay in the charity sector, especially when starting at the bottom of the ladder. The lowest point was speaking to a specialist agency that refused to meet me, claiming they knew all about me from my CV and background. It turned out they had me, and others like me, in a 'special category' waiting for the right chief executive position to become available. They had made huge and incorrect assumptions about my job and salary expectations. Fortunately, two agencies had the good grace to meet me and give me the opportunity to explain why I was determined to make the move to the charity sector. In short, it was not an easy transition!

Charities have to be managed and run on a commercial basis. The same levels of professionalism are required within the not-for-profit sector for a charity to be successful as are needed for a corporate to compete successfully in its market.

CV clinic

CVs are often your first point of contact with a potential new employer, so it's important to get yours right. If you are new to the world of work, include examples of how your training or volunteering experiences will be useful for the job you are applying for. If you are already working in the private or public sector, emphasise any previous experience related to fundraising such as marketing or sales. The skills acquired in such roles are a useful passport to your new job in fundraising.

Recruitment agencies can provide help with preparing CVs; many offer free information sheets or advice on their website.

i *See* Where to look for jobs *section (above) for information about recruitment agencies and websites*

CV tips

- List your key achievements, with specific examples of targets achieved, budget managed etc at the top of your CV. Forget the banal ones like 'works well with others' and don't be modest. Good examples for corporate candidates include '250% increase in revenue over two years' and 'achieved top distributor in Europe'.
- A recent holistic massage course may have changed your life but keep it for the interests and hobbies section. Don't distract from your relevant experience by listing unrelated and potentially misleading items at the top of your CV – it could make you look unfocused.
- Promote any voluntary work you have done and describe each activity, the amount of money raised and any skills developed. This shows your commitment to the sector.
- 'Brand' yourself as the type of candidate that charities will want. Be specific about describing the activities that are relevant to the job description and person specification and also give examples. Have different paragraphs and bullet points ready to adapt and customise your CV and application forms to each individual role.
- Don't forget to check your spelling – 'not for prophet sector' and 'attention to detial' will not impress potential employers. Ask someone else to proof read your CV to spot any errors you might have missed.
- Keep CVs to a maximum of two pages.

Source: Charity People

Content and structure

Your CV is both a sales tool and a formal information document. Remember that non-work experiences can show a lot about a person. A stint spent travelling may have improved your self-management skills; caring for a family member or friend demonstrates dedication to a cause; volunteering on an environmental project may have given you experience of working as a team.

Sample CV

The sections below are listed in the order that they are generally expected to appear on a CV.

Personal profile

Who you are, what you offer, what you want to do and where you want to go.

Use positive words – *adaptable* administrator, *flexible* PA, *confident* graduate, *experienced* corporate account manager, *creative* marketer etc.

Example:

A confident and mature graduate with 5 years marketing experience and a postgraduate marketing diploma, possessing excellent analytical skills and creative flair which have been successfully combined in a sales focused direct marketing role. Having proven project management ability and voluntary fundraising experience, I am now seeking the new challenge of a professional fundraising role in the charity sector.

Skills	Typing, computer packages, languages
Employment	List chronologically
	Demonstrate your skills and abilities
Achievements	Use positive words – organised, managed, achieved
Professional skills	Marketing/finance/IT skills
Volunteering	List same as employment
Education	Highest qualification first, including results
Additional skills	Make this interesting to the recruiter, or relevant to the position you are applying for

Source: Charity People

Covering letters and application forms

Most of the tips in the CV apply to covering letters and application forms too. Be specific and succinct and always highlight the most relevant experience and skills first.

When posting or emailing your CV, either in response to a particular job advert or on spec to enquire about vacancies, remember to send a covering letter. It's important to outline clearly what your key skills are and the type of work you believe you can do for them.

Recruitment agencies will request an up-to-date CV when you contact them. They will then send it to potential employers who may then ask you to fill in their standard application form.

When applying to a charity directly, you will find that most use application forms for equal opportunities purposes, so that information is presented in a standard fashion. The blank page asking you to explain how your experience and skills fit the post is the most important element of the form – and usually takes the longest to complete. One consultant advises that you list each category in the person specification on the left and match it directly with at least one example of how you have demonstrated that skill in the past.

Sample job descriptions and person specifications

Section 2 outlines some of the skills needed for fundraising jobs and typical work activities. This information is usually contained in the job description and person specification for the position you are applying for.

The job description includes information about the main purpose of the position; details of who you will report to or have responsibility for; main job activities and key responsibilities. The person specification outlines the qualifications, skills, experience and personal qualities required for the job. Some of these are essential; others will be desirable.

The information contained in the following examples is taken from real job descriptions and person specifications.

Director of development

Salary	£50,000–£55,000
Reports to	Chief executive
Responsible for	Head of marketing and public affairs; head of fundraising; PA/executive assistant
Main purpose of job	To develop and implement strategic planning to:

- maximise income through creative strategic partnerships, innovative and conventional fundraising techniques from all relevant statutory, corporate, trust and foundation sources, from major donors, individual committed and ad-hoc donors, lottery funds, events, trading activities, advertising and all other agreed sources
- market the charity and its services and products to agreed key stakeholders
- communicate agreed aims, objectives and values internally and externally and influence the national policy agenda in our areas of expertise and service delivery

Key responsibilities	Planning for income generation
	Implementation, monitoring and evaluation
	General management
	External and internal relationships
	Fundraising development
	Business development
	Departmental planning

Person specification

Formal qualifications	Graduate calibre
Experience	At least five years successful income generation management responsibility in one or more significant organisations.
	Successful record in developing and implementing marketing strategy for at least one multi-activity organisation.
	Experience of handling public relations and the media

	Successful record in building relationships with the corporate sector.
	Proven record of controlling large budgets.
	Experience in managing and promoting a charity brand.
	Successful experience of working with non-executive trustees, council or board.
	Experience in successfully leading and managing a substantial team in the achievement of their objectives.
Skills/abilities	A strategic thinker with vision and drive.
	Articulate in writing and speech, including preparing formal papers and speaking on public occasions.
	Able to operate effectively under pressure.
	Persuasive and diplomatic at all levels, at ease socially.
	Well organised director, delegator, and motivator: an inclusive team leader.
	A facilitator and co-ordinator.
	Ability to manage 'political' issues, national and international.
	IT-literate with an understanding of management information systems.
	Ability to understand complex legal and operational issues.
	Awareness of campaigning process.
Personal qualities	Understanding of and commitment to the voluntary sector and appreciation of its values.
	Commitment to the charity's culture, which includes consultative working practices and transparency and inclusion.
	Integrity and discretion.
	Authoritative, confident and decisive.
	Able to travel in the UK.

Corporate and trusts development manager

Salary £41,000

Reports to Head of fundraising

Responsible for Corporate and trusts team of six staff

Main purpose of job

To:

- devise and implement an ongoing three year strategy for corporate and trusts team

- ensure the team achieves its annually agreed income target from companies and trusts

- develop and sustain effective relationships with key corporate and trust contacts in order to maximise support to the charity in all areas and not just through fundraising.

Key responsibilities	Devises three-year strategy to ensure short and long term income targets are achieved and risks are minimised.
	Overall responsibility for raising annually agreed income target from companies and trusts.
	Takes personal responsibility for an annually agreed income target of £250,000.
	Oversees research into new market sectors and implements appropriate fundraising strategy.

Person specification

Education and qualifications	Degree or equivalent
Experience	
Essential	Minimum 5 years corporate fundraising experience.
	Minimum 3 years people management experience.
	Experience of managing income and expenditure budgets.
	Good track record of bringing in targeted income.
	Previous experience within a busy and fast moving environment.
	Experience of working in cross-departmental teams.

Desirable	Previous experience of leading a small-medium sized team.
	Experience of working with volunteers.
	Understanding of charity legislation as it applies to fundraising.

Special skills and knowledge

Essential	Strong communication skills (both written and verbal).
	Strong organisational skills, with ability to plan, prioritise and meet deadlines.
	Presentation skills.
	IT skills, particularly Word, Excel, Powerpoint 2.
	Able to manage staff with varying levels of experience.
	Networking skills.
Desirable	Knowledge of fundraising databases, particularly Alms.
	Personality and disposition.
	Approachable.
	Ability to coach others.
	Enthusiastic, innovative and creative.
	Special circumstances.
	Able to attend meetings out of normal office hours as required by the needs of the role (approximately three weekends per year).

Corporate partnerships assistant

Salary   £18,800

Reports to   Corporate partnerships developer

Main purpose of job

To:

- provide a support service to employees within the corporate partnership developer's accounts
- take responsibility for day to day account management of specific projects within these accounts
- help achieve the team's financial and non-financial objectives.

Key responsibilities

Account management, including the planning and evaluation of activities for corporate partner plus any new business secured or managed by the corporate partnerships developer.

Communicate fundraising information and procedures effectively to employees both verbally and in written documents (including letters and fundraising packs) to ensure that employees have clarity on all aspects of the fundraising campaign, as well as being highly motivated to get involved.

Respond to telephone enquiries from supporter employees with enthusiasm and knowledge, providing the highest standard of customer service to ensure supporter motivation and satisfaction.

Liaison with distribution centres, fulfilment houses and volunteers to ensure timely and accurate delivery of all fundraising materials to supporter employees within agreed deadlines in order to maximise fundraising opportunities and to maintain the confidence of employee supporters.

Maintain and develop highly organised administrative systems (for either ongoing activities or for specific campaigns) to maximise the efficiency of designated accounts and to provide excellent customer service.

Regularly update Raiser's Edge with non-financial corporate information, such as address changes and mailing preferences and also maintain corporate paper files to ensure complete and accurate corporate records are readily available.

Updating corporate sections of website and writing copy for in-house publications.

Person specification

Knowledge, skills and experience

Essential

- 18 months experience of fundraising or marketing
- Experience of customer or client service
- Excellent communication and interpersonal skills
- Excellent grasp of written English
- Ability to prioritise a number of activities
- High standard of organisation
- High standard of self motivation
- Good eye for detail
- Computer literate
- Excellent administration skills
- Flexible approach to work
- Good team working skills
- Degree or equivalent

Desirable

- Experience of supervising others at work
- Experience of Raisers Edge database
- Experience of writing for different types of audience/publication

Interviews

Preparation is key to a successful interview and it's vital to find out all you can about your potential employer in advance. Get the annual report and check the website if it has one. You should find out as much as you can about the organisation's current fundraising activities and funding sources – government grants, legacies etc. If it runs a project or service, visit this too. Search the internet for other information about the organisation.

Most voluntary sector interviews are now governed by equal opportunities guidelines; some organisations interpret this more stringently than others. Every candidate will be asked the same questions by a panel (usually three people) and interviewers will fill in a matrix that can be compared afterwards. This style of interview can be a culture shock for people switching from the corporate sector. Some organisations won't ask follow-up questions either, as this could be viewed as giving an unfair advantage to certain candidates.

Recruitment for fundraising roles usually involves two interviews, even for junior level posts. Often you will be asked to do a presentation where the panel pretends to be a potential donor – perhaps a company or a wealthy individual. This will give you the opportunity to demonstrate strategic thinking, how you formulate plans and how well you can communicate both with potential donors and your future colleagues.

Remember that you are interviewing the organisation to find out if it is the best place for you, just as much as the interview panel is looking for the best candidate. It's important to ask questions when you are given

---

Common interview 'gaffes' – read and avoid!

- Lack of research on the particular charity/ fundraising department/fundraising sector/fundraising in general.
- Not wearing appropriate interview clothing.
- Being late.
- Asking about salary and benefits – wait until the interviewers introduce it or even until you are actually offered the job, when you will be in a much stronger negotiating position.
- Not conducting yourself in a professional manner. Wait until you've got the job to make friends with colleagues; don't try to do it in the interview.
- Arrogance. Show that you are willing to learn and that you have as much to gain by getting this job as they have by employing you.

Source: Kage Partnership

the opportunity at the end of the interview; make sure that they demonstrate your knowledge and interest in the role.

Asking about the plans for the fundraising department, while showing that you already have some knowledge, can be a good starting point. For example: 'I notice that you raise a major part of your income through corporate fundraising. Will future fundraising strategy continue this or is the aim to diversify more into new areas?'

Criminal record checks

If the fundraising job involves regular contact with children or other vulnerable people, the organisation will require any successful applicant to undertake a standard or an enhanced disclosure check through the Criminal Records Bureau. However, a criminal record may not necessarily bar you from employment. The Criminal Records Bureau (www.crb.gov.uk) has more information about disclosure and how the information you provide is treated.

Hopefully, this section will have provided you with plenty of practical tips and resources for researching fundraising as a career and finding the right job for you. So all that remains is to wish you the best of luck with your job hunting and a long and successful career in fundraising!

Section 5

Getting ahead

Introduction

So you've got your job in fundraising. Now how do you develop it into a career?

As the case studies in this guide show, there is no single route into a successful career in fundraising. There are however several options available to fundraisers looking to improve their skills, broaden their experience and increase their knowledge.

The good news is that fundraisers are in demand. According to the Futureskills 2003 report – published by the Voluntary Sector National Training Organisation – a quarter of voluntary organisations have a fundraising skills gap. Fundraising was cited by 43% of respondents as being more important to their organisation than it had been in the previous three years. Meanwhile over a quarter (26.5%) identified restrictions associated with project funding as a key challenge.

Charities are now competing with universities, arts organisations and NHS trusts to attract experienced fundraisers. At a time when fundraising is a growth sector, there is a shortage of quality candidates, particularly with specialist skills in areas such as trust fundraising.

The Institute of Fundraising's 2004 membership survey shows that an increasing number of people are choosing to carve out a career in fundraising. Over a quarter (26.5%) have worked in fundraising for between six and 10 years and nearly one in five (18.1%) have been fundraisers for between 11 and 15 years.

Most fundraisers have been in their current post for less than 10 years. Around a third (32.7%) have been in post for one to two years, over a quarter (26.1%) for between three and five years. Only a small number (6.3%) have had the same job for 11 years or more. The vast majority (82.7%) said that they had never been made redundant.

Professional development

Professional development is a key part of equipping yourself with the skills needed to progress in fundraising. For the purposes of this guide, we have used the term 'professional development' to cover formal qualifications in fundraising, training in specific areas of fundraising or related areas and informal routes, such as networking and attending events.

With all forms of professional development, it is important to first decide what you want to achieve. Do you:

- want a professional qualification, to demonstrate to your current – and future – employer that you are qualified to a particular industry level?
- need to acquire new skills in a particular area of fundraising, with a view to changing jobs or because your current role is evolving?
- wish to develop existing skills, perhaps with a view to promotion?
- want to learn from your peers in an informal environment?

Once you have established exactly why and what you want to develop, the next step is to assess the time you have available. If your time is limited, you might prefer one-off training courses or a qualification that requires study over a period of a year or more. Depending on your employer, you may be able to study part time or take off a block of time to complete training. If the only free time you have is in the evenings or at weekends, distance learning or online study might be your best option. These options may also be more suitable if you are not located near to the training provider or college running your chosen course.

Funding is another important factor. Your organisation's training policy will probably specify what it will and will not fund. You may need to demonstrate how your employer's investment in a particular training course or activity will impact on your performance and on the fundraising department as a whole.

Finally, you'll need to assess which course or activity is most appropriate for your experience. Some courses may have minimum entry requirements, such as a certain amount of time in fundraising or a degree in a related discipline.

ⓘ *The Institute of Fundraising (www.institute-of-fundraising.org.uk) can provide further information about professional training and development in fundraising.*

ⓘ *For further information about fundraising and professional development, visit www.fundraising.co.uk or www.volresource.org.uk*

Careerbank

Careerbank is an initiative of the Institute of Fundraising. It is designed to help fundraisers manage their career by offering them a method of planning, developing and recording professional development. Careerbank has been designed to reflect and help all fundraisers but will initially be circulated to all individual members of the Institute of Fundraising.

Members receive a 'fundraising career pathway', which they can use to record, plan and assess any development activity, such as attending a seminar or training course; reading; committee work or on-the-job learning. The pathway is divided into four sections, represented by an interlocking jigsaw with each piece symbolising a progression in an area of a fundraising career. Each section of the framework contains a list of skills and aptitudes, commensurate with each phase of a typical fundraising career.

Fundraisers can map themselves against this framework and use it to identify any skills gaps they may need to build upon before moving on to the next phase. The mapping exercise demonstrates areas in a fundraising career that each fundraiser should aspire to achieve. It has been designed to reflect that a career path is not a simple journey from A to B. For example, a fundraiser may have considerable management skills but no practical fundraising experience.

ⓘ *Further information from the Institute of Fundraising at www.institute-of-fundraising.org.uk*

Qualifications

Fundraising qualifications

Attaining a professional qualification in fundraising will demonstrate your ability to successfully manage the fundraising process and show your understanding of the sector. Recruitment consultants suggest that the combination of qualifications and training with fundraising experience shows a high degree of commitment to the profession and could set you apart from other candidates when looking for your next job.

S/NVQs in fundraising

National Vocational Qualifications (NVQs) or Scottish Vocational Qualifications (SVQs) are work-related qualifications that recognise a person's skills, experience and knowledge. They are based on national occupational standards (NOS), which describe what competent people in a particular occupation are expected to be able to do. There are five levels of S/NVQ, with level 4 approximately the same level as an undergraduate degree and level 5 equivalent to a postgraduate degree.

Work is currently underway to develop S/NVQs in fundraising following the publication in February 2004 of national occupational standards (NOS) in fundraising. Published by the Voluntary Sector National Training Organisation (VSNTO), these standards will form the basis of S/NVQs at levels 2, 3 and 4 for managing fundraising.

It is anticipated that larger charities and not-for-profit organisations will apply to an awarding body offering these qualifications to become approved centres in their own right.

The VSNTO is working with the Institute of Fundraising to ensure this project develops a qualification which can act as a stepping stone for those fundraisers who are interested in pursuing the Institute's own qualifications.

ⓘ *The VSNTO (www.vsnto.org.uk) has more information about the fundraising national occupational standards*

The Certificate in Fundraising Management
Institute of Fundraising (www.institute-of-fundraising.org.uk)

The Institute of Fundraising launched the Certificate in Fundraising Management (CiFM) in 1998 to offer fundraisers a professional qualification based on their fundraising competence. Over 870 Institute members have achieved, or are working towards, the qualification.

The CiFM is a competence-based programme and competencies are management focused and generic in nature. This means that those completing the certificate will have demonstrated their ability to successfully manage the fundraising process rather than having demonstrated knowledge of any particular fundraising technique or techniques.

The certificate comprises two modules:

- Module 1 Fundraising practice: focuses on the process involved in fundraising and identifies the skills and knowledge required to demonstrate basic fundraising practice
- Module 2 Managing fundraising: concerns the management of fundraising and fundraisers and links fundraising to the strategic aims of the organisation

Fundraisers can achieve the CiFM in two ways:

- Certificated training route: fundraisers can attend Institute-approved training courses that lead to the award of the CiFM (see below). These are offered by a range of partners, including universities and private training providers, and address the skills and knowledge required to complete either or both Module 1 and Module 2 of the certificate.
- Supported assessment route: fundraisers can develop a portfolio of evidence and submit it to the Institute for accreditation by one of its licensed assessors (see the Institute's website for a list of assessors).

A number of training courses offer fundraisers a route to achieving the CiFM. These include:

- The Fundraising Programme: The Foundation Course in Fundraising Practice (CiFM Module 1)
- The Projects Company: The Certificate in Fundraising Management (CiFM Module 2)
- Sheffield Hallam University: The Certificate in Fundraising Management (CiFM Module 1 & 2)
- Cass Business School: Postgraduate Diploma/MSc in Charity Marketing & Finance (CiFM Module 1 & 2)
- Open University: Winning Resources and Support (CiFM Module 1 & 2)
- Fundraising Training Limited: Fundraising trainee programme (CiFM Module 1)

- Professional Fundraising Consultancy: Certificate in Fundraising for Schools (CiFM Module 1)

ⓘ》 *A full list of training providers and licensed assessors is available from the Institute's website at www.institute-of-fundraising.org.uk*

ⓘ》 *See* **Directory** *for details of certificated training providers*

Most fundraisers on the standard route should be able to complete within six months. All Institute of Fundraising licensees provide individually tailored programmes so costs do vary. As a general guide, the standard route to the certificate will cost in the region of £750 to £1,000. The certificated training route will cost from £1,500 to upwards of £2,000, depending on the provider.

The Institute of Fundraising recommends that you clarify the total costs of your chosen route with your provider before embarking on study.

Q&As

Q: *I have been a fundraiser for ten years. What route to gaining the CiFM would you recommend?*
A: The standard route is designed to allow experienced fundraisers to demonstrate their fundraising competence in an effective and efficient manner.
The certificate can be gained in around six months by working with a licensed assessor and utilising fundraising materials that can be up to five years old, to develop and submit a portfolio of evidence.

Q: *I would like to sign up for the CiFM but I am not an Institute of Fundraising member. Does this matter?*
A: To be awarded the certificate you must have been an associate member for at least 12 months. The Institute recommends that non-members join when they register for the certificate.

Q: *After several years in marketing in the private sector I am now involved in fundraising. Can you advise me on the best way to approach the CiFM?*
A: Many of the skills developed during other careers are transferable to fundraising and to the certificate. However, the CiFM is a fundraising qualification and as such requires you to demonstrate specialist fundraising skills. You might consider the training options leading towards the certificate. Equally, for many professionals, the standard route would provide sufficient support for you to achieve this qualification.

Q: *I am hoping to become a fundraiser. Can I complete the CiFM to help make the career change?*
A: As the certificate is a competence-based programme you will need to have the opportunity to translate theory into practice, whether in a paid or unpaid capacity. You cannot achieve the CiFM by simply attending a course. Those who are not currently employed as a fundraiser are advised to build their experience as a volunteer.

Certified Fund Raising Executive

The Association of Fundraising Consultants (www.afc.org.uk)

The AFC is to offer a UK version of the Certified Fund Raising Executive (CFRE), an internationally recognised credential for senior professional fundraisers. The CFRE is held by over 6,000 fundraisers in the USA, Canada, New Zealand and Australia.

Candidates for the CFRE must demonstrate at least five years of fund-raising experience. In addition there are specific requirements related to professional development and fundraising performance. The CFRE is awarded on the basis of a written application and written examination.

ⓘ *Further information about the CFRE from www.afc.org.uk or www.cfre.org.uk*

Postgraduate diploma and MSc – charity marketing and fundraising

Cass Business School, City University (www.cass.city.ac.uk)

This course is designed for managers working at a senior level in charities and not-for profit organisations who wish to gain a recognised academic qualification and the Institute of Fundraising's Certificate in Fundraising Management. Students undertake four core modules, followed by two specialist subject modules. The courses are taught over 13 months for the postgraduate diploma with a further six months of supervised personal research leading to the presentation of a 10,000-word written project to attain the master's degree.

On completion of the postgraduate diploma, the Institute of Fundraising will grant its Certificate in Fundraising Management. The fee for the postgraduate diploma is £3,800; for the MSc a further £2,500 is payable.

Postgraduate certificate, diploma and MSc – charity marketing and fundraising

London South Bank University (www.lsbu.ac.uk)

This course (subject to review in 2004) is aimed at fundraisers and marketing managers working within charities and voluntary organisations. It is divided into self-contained course units that provide a pathway from certificate through diploma to the award of a master's degree.

The postgraduate certificate takes one academic year to complete. Course units cover marketing and meeting customer need, fundraising, charity accounting and finance, and strategic charity marketing. The diploma is achieved over two years of academic study, consisting of the four certificate units plus three further units from human resource management, voluntary sector financial management, applied charity law and research methods. The master's degree adds a course unit in research methods followed by individual supervised research study leading to a dissertation.

Course units can be completed by half day into evening study, one day per week, or by means of block release, which involves two full-day blocks on six occasions spaced evenly throughout the academic year. Fees in 2003-04 for the certificate and first year of the master's and diploma were £1,460 and £2,080 for the second year of the master's and diploma.

Other relevant courses from LSBU include:

- MBA (Charity management): a general management qualification, with charity management as one of six specialist routes. Taught at South Bank Business School as a two-year, part-time programme, on two evenings per week.
- MVA in nonprofit and voluntary sector management: new master's in voluntary administration combining professional and practitioner involvement supported by contemporary research.

Winning resources and support
Open University (www.open.ac.uk)

This six-month course focuses on the skills and knowledge necessary for successful fundraising and leads to the Institute of Fundraising's Certificate in Fundraising Management, subject to membership conditions. The course is for people working in not-for-profit organisations whose responsibilities include fundraising, or for people who have some experience in fundraising on a voluntary basis and would like to improve their skills in this area.

Course content includes an overview of the roles and responsibilities of fundraisers and a guide to the necessary skills and competences. It also covers fundraising communications; supporters, donors and customers; sourcing and managing resources, and fundraising strategy.

The current fee is £875. Successful participants will be awarded the CiFM after one year's membership of the Institute of Fundraising.

The Open University also offers the professional certificate in management – public and non-profit organisations. This is a foundation course (NVQ level 4) for new, general or middle managers in the not-for-profit sector. The course covers recruitment, motivation, teamwork and leadership; how to interpret and use financial and other information, and marketing and quality management concepts. There are no entry requirements for the certificate, but personal knowledge and experience of managing in an organisation is desirable.

The 12-month course includes a residential school or an 18-day online equivalent and has an end-of-course examination. The current fee is £2,230.

Personal perspective: Richard Mountford

Job: Development manager

Organisation: Animal Aid

Age: 43

To see the abolition of vivisection and factory farming is my personal long-term aim. And my current role as development manager is flexible enough that I can still get involved in campaigning even though the main focus is on managing a fundraising team of two full-time staff and a number of volunteers.

For 15 years before I took this salaried position I campaigned for a local Animal Aid group in Birmingham on a voluntary basis, while working for the Inland Revenue and then as a business and psychology teacher at a sixth form college. One of the main successes we achieved in Birmingham was persuading the council to draw up a charter abolishing the use of animals in circuses and fairs.

Animal Aid does not have charitable status, which means we don't benefit from tax breaks like Gift Aid, or receive any government funding. This makes fundraising even more crucial but it also allows us to retain an independent voice for campaigning. Database or direct marketing is the main focus of our fundraising – sending out appeals to secure committed giving and then increase the average amount given.

Training is crucial for anyone switching to a fundraising career. I found the Institute of Fundraising certificate useful for reviewing achievements and planning ahead and I am also taking the Institute of Legacy Management certificate of competence.

Personal perspective: Charlotte Langley

Job: Director of fundraising

Organisation: Guy's & St Thomas' Charitable Foundation and NHS Trust

Age: 41

I've been involved with fundraising all my life. As a very young child I took part in sponsored swims and later volunteered for the International Red Cross and Mother Theresa's Missionaries of Charity.

After working for an antique and art dealer for two and half years, I got a job as a 'girl Friday' at the Muscular Dystrophy Campaign where I was involved in all forms of fundraising. After that, I took a fundraising and PR role at the British Executive Services Overseas then moved to Leonard Cheshire where I advised 143 volunteer committees on fundraising matters.

Dealing with high level people and speaking to a wide range of people knowledgeably, were key tasks in my next two jobs. I was associate director of development in charge of the alumni programme at London Business School and then director of development at the Prince of Wales Institute of Architecture.

After that, as director of fundraising for the Parkinson's Society, I gained experience of working within a membership organisation. While in my next post as director of marketing and communications for the Elizabeth Finn Trust, there was a steep learning curve about marketing in the independent care home sector.

In my current role as joint director of fundraising for the Guy's and St Thomas' Charitable Foundation and the NHS Trust, my personal challenge is to reach the £10m target for the Evelina Appeal this year. And the next challenge will be to explore funding opportunities to meet Guy's and St Thomas' new clinical service strategy.

Other professional qualifications

A number of other professional bodies offer qualifications in disciplines related to fundraising. These include:

- The Chartered Institute of Marketing (www.cim.co.uk) offers an introductory certificate in marketing, certificate in marketing, advanced certificate in marketing and postgraduate diploma in marketing
- Institute of Direct Marketing (www.theidm.co.uk) offers a certificate in direct marketing and diploma in direct and interactive marketing

ⓘ *See listing in* **Directory** *for contact details*

5.3

Training

Fundraisers work in a competitive environment and success relies on having the right skills and experience for the job. It's no longer optional to keep up-to-date with the latest fundraising trend or technique; it is increasingly central to professional and organisational success.

The majority of fundraisers say their employers invest in their development through training. Over three quarters (78%) of respondents in the Institute's 2004 membership survey say this is the main way their organisation supports them, followed by appraisal (68.7%) and supervision (54.9%). Over three quarters (76.6%) have undertaken some form of fundraising training since entering the sector, while over a third (37.9%) have received marketing training and just under a third (28.2%) have had training in financial management. Popular areas of fundraising training include corporate, major gifts/donors and trusts. The most common professional qualification is the Institute's Certificate in Fundraising Management.

Training providers

A number of specialist training organisations and individual trainers offer fundraising training (see below). Councils for Voluntary Service (CVS) and local authorities may also run courses. Training courses can be expensive so it is worth checking out discounts through membership organisations (e.g. Institute of Fundraising members receive 10% off courses in the Fundraising Programme) or considering group training, if a course is relevant to other fundraisers within your organisation. The Institute's Training for Business service offers fundraising training for 10 or more delegates.

In addition to training in specific areas of fundraising, you might also find it useful to undertake training in:

- data protection
- employment law
- equal opportunities
- event management
- financial management
- health and safety
- IT

- internet fundraising
- marketing
- managing volunteers
- media
- presentation skills
- public relations
- recruitment and selection
- report writing
- strategic planning

ⓘ *See* **Directory** *for a list of training providers offering fundraising courses*

Funding for training

The following organisations offer information or assistance with funding for training:

- The Charities Aid Foundation's annual grantmaking programme includes a Fast Track Fund that offers grants of up to £600 to UK charities for fundraising training
- The Open University sometimes helps with the costs of course fees via the Financial Award Fund
- Learn Direct, a government-sponsored online learning network, offers advice on a range of courses and options for helping with fees

ⓘ *See* Directory *for contact details*

Training courses

A large number of other organisations provide courses of interest to fundraisers. The Directory at the end of this guide provides details of popular courses and training providers.

They include:

The Fundraising Programme (www.dsc.org.uk/charitytraining)

A joint initiative run by the Institute of Fundraising and the Directory of Social Change (DSC), this programme offers training for all fundraisers, from basic skills for new entrants to advanced courses that lead to the Institute's Certificate in Fundraising Management (CiFM). Training is offered at four levels: introductory level for those who are new to fundraising or a particular area of fundraising; intermediate level for fundraisers wanting to develop and evaluate existing skills; practitioner level for practising fundraisers requiring an intense, high level introduction to specialist areas, and advanced level for those who manage the fundraising function.

Effective fundraising, a level one course in the programme, is the most relevant for new starters as it offers a broad-based introduction to the techniques of basic fundraising. Other areas covered by the programme include trusts, companies, legacies, statutory funding, major gifts, special events, strategy development and law.

The programme's route to the CiFM is based around two courses – the foundation course in fundraising practice and managing fundraising. Successful completion of these courses and their assignments leads to the CiFM, subject to Institute membership.

An Introduction to Fundraising
(www.institute-of-fundraising.org.uk)
This is an accredited training programme designed to meet the needs of those who are new to fundraising or for whom fundraising is a small part of their role including volunteers, trustees and service deliverers. Fundraising organisations can buy the programme for delivery as part of their own training programmes, staff inductions or as a way of introducing staff, volunteers or trustees to fundraising.

Certificate in fundraising for schools
(www.pfconsultancy.co.uk)
This is a training and accreditation programme for those who are already, or intend to become, development or fundraising directors in schools. The programme is accredited by the University of Central Lancashire and the Institute of Fundraising.

The course caters for those who are already established as school fundraisers and require further training or accreditation, for new school development directors or fundraising officers, and for heads, bursars or other senior staff who need to take a leading fundraising role within their school. Previous delegates come from a wide range of secondary schools in the independent and state sectors.

The course covers fundraising strategy, developing support, major gifts and fundraising appeals. The course takes place twice a year and requires 200 hours of learning, usually completed within 12 months.

The National Arts Fundraising School
(www.managementcentre.co.uk)
Run through the Management Centre, this six-day intensive programme is aimed at fundraisers in arts and other cultural organisations, such as marketing managers, development officers,

communications directors, administrators, general managers, artistic directors, local authority arts officers, and festival organisers.

The course covers a wide range of areas including research, promotional material, lottery funding, legacies, sponsorship, proposal writing and tax breaks.

The Management Centre also runs courses in securing business sponsorship and influencing skills for fundraisers.

The Institute of Legacy Management Certificate of Competence (www.ilmnet.org)

Designed by the College of Law together with practising legacy officers, this course is aimed at legacy officers or administrators looking for an understanding of legacy management up to intermediate level.

The Charities Aid Foundation (www.cafonline.org)

CAF runs conferences, seminars and workshops on tax-effective giving, including payroll giving. It also organises an annual conference, highlighting recent funding and political trends in the voluntary sector.

Personal perspective: Laura McVeigh

Job: Planning and development officer

Organisation: The Place To Be

Age: 29

I did a degree in languages at Cambridge then joined a new media company as sales and marketing manager. After a year and a half, I moved to a publishing companies group where my job involved setting up new media for marketing and production. I stayed there for about four years, at the end of which I'd realised that it just wasn't for me.

So I decided to do an MSc in global politics at Birkbeck College and got involved in student volunteering, with Save the Children and Unicef. I realised that I was very interested in this sector and felt that my sales and marketing skills were really transferable. When I started applying for jobs in the sector, I targeted children's charities rather than going for the blanket approach.

Since September 2003, I've been working at The Place to Be, a charity that provides emotional and therapeutic support to children in schools. Because it is a small charity, the job takes in a mix of things: making large funding applications, managing corporate partnerships, overseeing payroll giving and setting up online fundraising – where my new media experience is useful.

When I moved to the voluntary sector, my concerns were that you wouldn't get the training and support you need. But my employer has been excellent about training, sponsoring me to do the Institute of Fundraising certificate and sending me on appropriate courses.

My job is flexible as I can work from home and am often out visiting projects. There's an awful lot of scope and potential in the voluntary sector to develop your career. You might need to take a drop in salary but once you go beyond middle management, the salaries are much better.

I also do voluntary fundraising for the Young Fabians, a think tank, which is helping me develop skills in corporate sponsorship, generating advertising revenue and running a team of members.

There is still a perception that fundraising is the easiest part of the voluntary sector to get into. I don't think it's an easy career choice but if you are very stubborn, a good listener and can put yourself in the funders' shoes, you can really develop. And you really have to care for the cause so you can put your case forward.

Other professional development

Networking

Previous positions and past achievements demonstrate your fundraising experience but learning from your peers is an essential part of continuing professional development. Networking plays an important role in helping fundraisers keep up-to-date with sector developments and share experiences of what works – and what doesn't.

If you want to meet and learn from other fundraisers working in the same field of fundraising, a good starting point is the Institute of Fundraising's special interest groups (SIG). These offer fundraisers a forum for exchanging ideas, learning and job opportunities, through email groups and events, often featuring external speakers. There are currently groups covering corporate fundraising, Christian organisations, committed giving, diversity, hospitals, IT, major donors, payroll giving, statutory and trusts.

There are also separate groups for fundraising consultants and researchers while fundraisers in Scotland can participate in groups covering committed giving, corporate and trusts.

For local networking, the Institute's regional groups cover Anglia, Chilterns, London, Midlands, north east, north west, south east, south west, Wessex and Yorkshire. Groups are also active in Northern Ireland, Scotland and Wales. Like the special interest groups, these host talks, seminars and informal events for fundraisers working in the same region.

Networking via email and the internet has become a popular and effective way for fundraisers to learn and develop. One of the most active resources is the UK Fundraising Forum (www.fundraising.co.uk/forum), which since 1996 has helped fundraisers to share expertise and debate. This has now spawned several email discussion lists on various fundraising specialisms, including direct marketing, legacies and new media.

Company Solutions (www.companysolutions.biz) hosts a number of discussion forums for fundraisers, covering subjects such as community fundraising and volunteer management. The voluntary sector information website VolResource, (www.volresource.org.uk) has a discussion forum on Yahoo! Groups and also lists other online forums for the sector.

Attending training courses, seminars and conferences also gives you the chance to meet fellow fundraisers and pick up news about other organisations' activities and job opportunities. In addition to the Institute's annual National Convention (see below), the training event Charityfair (www.dsc.org.uk/charityfair) and recruitment fair Forum3 (www.forum3.co.uk) offer networking opportunities. Contact the professional body covering your fundraising sector for details of events and networking information.

ⓘ》 *See below for information about events*

ⓘ》 *See* **Directory** *for details of professional bodies*

Conferences and events

Developing your professional knowledge relies on keeping up to date with the latest fundraising developments. As well as undertaking individual training courses, you will also benefit from attending events that offer a wider perspective of the sector. Such events can provide you with information on new fundraising techniques, target markets and sector research. They also offer valuable 'time out' from your day job and will help you to maintain an innovative approach to fundraising.

Useful events include:

Institute of Fundraising National Convention (www.institute-of-fundraising.org.uk)
An annual three-day learning and networking event for fundraisers, this event includes plenaries, workshops and sessions for all levels of experience plus a varied social programme to facilitate networking. It also offers specialist advice to fundraisers on personal and career development.

Charityfair (www.dsc.org.uk/charityfair)
An annual two-day learning and skills event organised by the Directory of Social Change, Charityfair provides workshops, masterclasses and introductory sessions on a range of voluntary sector issues including fundraising. It also features an exhibition of charities, statutory and commercial organisations.

Forum3 (www.forum3.co.uk)
This is an annual recruitment and volunteering fair for the not-for-profit sector. In addition to exhibitors from the voluntary sector, there are sessions on fundraising, personal development and volunteering. Advice and information on fundraising is provided by the Institute of Fundraising, Directory of Social Change and forum3 organiser Charity People.

CAF annual conference (www.cafonline.org)

Organised by the Charities Aid Foundation (CAF), this event provides a round-up of the latest research and thinking related to funding the voluntary sector and tax effective giving. The event also includes an exhibition.

NCVO annual conference (www.ncvo-vol.org.uk)

Organised by the National Council of Voluntary Organisations (NCVO), this event highlights key trends, developments and good practice in the voluntary sector through seminars and workshops. NCVO also organises an annual research conference, which offers insights into operations and funding.

In addition to attending events, you might want to contribute as a speaker or volunteer to chair a discussion. Presenting to fellow fundraisers at seminars, workshops and other events is another key element of professional development.

Many events organisers look for potential speakers up to a year in advance so contact them early to find out about opportunities to share your experience and skills with other fundraisers.

❶❯ *See* **Directory** *for full details and other events*

Awards

Official recognition for your achievements as a fundraiser can help to promote both your organisation and your career. There are a number of sector awards schemes that recognise fundraisers' efforts.

The largest is the Professional Fundraising/Institute of Fundraising awards (www.professionalfundraising.co.uk), which highlights success and innovation in all areas of fundraising. The awards are open to charities, theatres, schools, arts organisations and hospitals, and there are categories for individual achievement.

The Charity Awards (www.charityawards.co.uk) and UK Charity Awards (www.charitytimes.com) also include personal achievement categories.

❶❯ *See* **Directory** *for full details and other fundraising awards*

Personal perspective: Janine Pemberton

Job: Account director

Organisation: Target Direct (direct marketing agency)

Age 31

I became interested in direct marketing while taking a marketing degree at the University of Teesside. I then spent five years working in-house for financial services companies, and took an Institute of Direct Marketing diploma, before joining a direct marketing agency in Cirencester.

I've worked with a number of charity and commercial clients during the two years I've been an account director at Target Direct, based in Cheltenham. Donor acquisition, awareness raising, volunteer recruitment and legacy direct marketing campaigns are some of the areas that I focus on with charity clients.

Spending 10 days in Malawi on a Water Aid supporters trip helped me to 'physically' understand the brand – the emotive effects of poverty and the importance of access to clean water. Charity brands aren't always tangible in the same way as a product like a tube of toothpaste and limited marketing budgets mean that you have to be innovative to deliver targets.

Working for an agency allows you to get a variety of different skills and the opportunity to work across a range of large and small clients. It's more challenging and exciting as you are part of lots of different teams and I get a real buzz when taking part in a pitch or 'wowing' clients with a brilliant end product.

Mentoring and job coaching

Mentoring is an activity where one individual provides voluntary support to another individual, on a formal or informal basis. A mentor can help a mentee to develop his or her professional career, through giving advice and acting as a sounding board for making decisions.

A mentor in a senior position within your organisation or in another organisation can help you to adjust to a new senior role or wider management responsibilities. Mentoring can take the form of informal face-to-face meetings, email communication or telephone sessions; frequency may range from once a week to monthly or ad hoc communication.

Some organisations promote mentoring as part of their professional development programme. If yours does not, you might be able to identify a potential mentor through networking (see above) or through the professional body for your fundraising sector. The Institute of Fundraising's special interest and regional groups are a good starting point for identifying potential mentors.

A number of private companies also offer mentoring services for fundraisers. These include Kew Quorum (www.kewquorum.co.uk) and 3rd Solutions (www.3rdsolutions.com).

ℹ️ *The National Mentoring Network (www.nmn.org.uk) provides information about mentoring activities and events*

A note of caution: before entering into any sort of mentoring or job-coaching arrangement, it is important that you are clear about what you hope to get out of the relationship and what is being offered. It is worth doing some research into the individual or company providing the service, and also speaking to their previous mentees for their opinions and experience.

Moving on

Fundraising offers a variety of career progression pathways. The Institute's 2004 membership survey found that many fundraisers expect to continue their career with their current employer. Over a third (37.7%) however want to move into a bigger role but do not mind if it is with a different cause.

What is your most desirable career progression scenario?

Same job for ever, happy where I am	15.6%
Same job, different charity	5.6%
Bigger job, same charity	12.2%
Bigger job, same cause	7.0%
Bigger job, any cause that I believe in	37.7%
Moving to another sector	7.5%
Other	14.3%

Source: Institute of Fundraising 2004 membership survey

Career progression

If you've joined at a junior level such as fundraising assistant, you may decide to continue your career within the organisation if it is large enough to offer suitable opportunities. Alternatively, you might decide to move on once you have one or two years' experience under your belt. Many voluntary organisations have flat management and organisational structures. While there may be more room for promotion opportunities or career development in larger charities, in a smaller one you might need to move out to move up.

It is common for fundraisers in smaller organisations to have responsibility for a whole range of fundraising activities. If you wish to specialise in a specific area, such as events or legacies, you may need to move to a larger charity with a bigger budget and separate fundraising department. So when you are considering where you want to work, it is important to think about your preferences for personal development.

In a larger organisation such as a national charity, there is plenty of scope after a year or so in post to take responsibility for a specific event or campaign. In a smaller organisation – a local arts centre or hospital trust for example – two or three years experience could secure you a post as a senior

My first job as a teacher in New Zealand equipped me with the planning and organisational skills I needed to become a part-time fundraiser while bringing up my children. I then became a fundraising consultant for an Australian company, working with clients such as the Salvation Army on capital campaigns using direct marketing.

I moved to the UK in 1990 and worked as a consultant on feasibility studies for capital campaigns and strategic planning. Coming from a different country and working for an Australian company was enormously helpful for this work. I then moved to a job as director of fundraising at Voluntary Service Overseas: it was the first time fundraising had had its own division so I was the first director. We were trying to triple income, working on high value donors. From having only managed two people before, I went to managing 30 plus but my consultancy experience had prepared me for working with teams and trustees.

I then took a career break when my husband took a job in Brazil. I worked as a volunteer there and completed an MBA by distance learning. I returned to the UK after three years and took a six-month contract as head of fundraising at English Heritage. It was a 'babysitting' job while the organisation made internal changes. From there I moved to RNID as executive director of fundraising, a big career step that involved a fundraising operation of £18m. I oversaw growth in the corporate area, including Barclays Bank's £1.3m involvement over four years.

As a result of this, I was seconded for six months as head of community affairs at Barclays on a maternity cover basis. I loved the different cultures: the company wanted to understand the charity sector better so it was a great opportunity to learn. I joined Action Planning as chief executive in 2003 and now use my fundraising, strategic planning and management experience to lead major fundraising projects for our clients and to help charities appoint chief executives and fundraising directors.

Sometimes you miss the passion of working for one charity but I love the fact that you can see such a broad range of organisations and can stand back with some perspective.

fundraiser or head of fundraising. If you decide to move into the commercial sector, this experience may help you to get a job as a brand manager, database manager, direct marketing manager or e-marketing manager.

Between five and 10 years experience coupled with proven management and business skills should enable you to work as a head of fundraising in a larger organisation or as a senior fundraising specialist. Here you might have the opportunity to take on other responsibilities such as human resources or strategic development. Leadership skills will equip you for a chief executive role, either in a fundraising organisation or commercial consultancy.

Consultancy work

Many experienced fundraisers decide to use their expertise in consultancy roles. Consultants work as individuals or through a consultancy to offer specialist skills and objective advice. As a consultant you might help an organisation to review a fundraising strategy, develop a new income stream or establish a capital fund. Consultancy work offers the advantages of working with a variety of causes or fundraising sectors and on time-limited projects.

Around 7% of respondents in the Institute's 2004 membership survey work as fundraising consultants, either through a consultancy company or on a freelance basis. Some of these work as interim managers, taking on the fundraising function at director level while an organisation recruits for a new, permanent member of staff or restructures. Several recruitment consultants now offer an interim manager placement service.

ⓘ See **Section 2** *for more on consultancy work*

ⓘ See **Directory** *for details of recruitment consultants and websites*

Job hunting resources

Before you start looking for your next job, it's important that you are clear about what you want to achieve. Are you looking for a more senior role in a different organisation? Do you want to build on your training to specialise? Or do you want the hands-on experience that a smaller fundraising organisation can offer?

Think about:

- the type of work you are seeking
- the fundraising sector (e.g charities, arts) you want to work in
- your salary expectations
- the geographical area in which you wish to work

- your skills and experience, gained either in a paid or voluntary capacity
- your career aspirations

Section 4 provides information about getting a job in fundraising and the resources available to jobhunters. These include:
- specialist recruitment consultants such as Charity Recruitment or Kingston Smith Executive Selection
- specialist press such as the Guardian's Media supplement, Professional Fundraising and Arts Professional
- minority press such as Caribbean Times and Jewish Chronicle
- recruitment websites such as Guardian Jobs
- recruitment events such as Forum3.

ℹ️ *See* **Section 4** *for more information about job hunting*

ℹ️ *See* **Directory** *for full details and more job hunting resources*

Guardian Jobmatch for fundraisers (jobs.guardian.co.uk/jobmatch)

Jobmatch for fundraisers is an online service from Guardian Unlimited, supported by the Institute of Fundraising, to match fundraisers and would-be fundraisers with those who need their skills.

Candidates can register their profile, outline their qualifications and experience and receive details by email of vacancies that match their skills, as well as viewing job opportunities on the site. Employers who sign up to the service can have their vacancies matched to candidates with the same skills and have the vacancy sent direct to relevant candidates.

The service enables jobseekers to search by specific fundraising role, charity, location or salary. To ensure privacy, the employer knows nothing about the jobseeker being sent the vacancy until he or she chooses to apply for the job. The jobseeker will tell the service to forward their profile to an employer when they receive a job they are interested in. At this point, the employer and jobseeker have been 'matched' and the application will continue in the normal way. Jobmatch is not a recruitment agency and no commission or fee is charged for contact or placement of jobseekers.

Sample jobseeker profile

Jobs: Fundraising manager/Fundraising co-ordinator

About me

Currently based in Madrid I have been working for three years as senior fundraising manager for IHRO (International Human Rights Organisation). I am keen to use the skills I have developed during my ten years of fundraising working in a variety of community and not-for-profit contexts.

Employment history

Senior fundraising manager IHRO (International Human Rights Organisation), 1998–present

Reporting to the head of fundraising I am responsible for managing a team of 10 fundraising officers, including two who are based in our Brussels office.

I have played a leading role, as internal facilitator, in the successful implementation of Investors in People.

I have made a significant contribution to organisational change through leading the expansion of our new international volunteer programme.

I led my team in achieving its target of raising an additional $2m between 2000 and 2002, in part through initiating a new sponsored events programme.

Fundraising officer, Refugee Support Group, 1993–1998

My responsibilities included coordinating and supporting a group of London-wide volunteers; organising direct mail and regional advertising campaigns and organising training events for local volunteers.

Voluntary, community and public service experience

1983–1995: active volunteer with Latin American Human Rights Committee
1990–1993: Elected member of national executive of above
1994–1998: School governor, local secondary school, London

ICT skills

Competency in word processing; spreadsheets; database administration and design; statistical analysis software.

Qualifications and accredited training

BSc Hons Business and Public Sector Strategy (1980)
Investors in People Internal Facilitator (September 1998)
Public Sector MBA (Open University, October 2002)

Anything else?

I am fluent in Spanish and French.

Recent training and development

Working with volunteers (European Council for Voluntary Organisations), 3 days, 2000.
Ongoing ICT training in database management and use of the internet.

Sectors

Children/young people
Human rights
International

Languages

French
Spanish

About the Institute
of Fundraising

Who we are

Founded 20 years ago, the Institute of Fundraising is a not-for-profit organisation based in London with national and regional offices. As well as being a membership organisation, our core activities are professional standards, policy development, training and events. The chief executive reports to a board of trustees elected from the membership.

Our mission

As a professional body the Institute seeks to represent all fundraisers. Our mission is to develop, promote and champion excellence in fundraising. Through our members and the best practice of fundraising, we seek to engage and influence at all relevant levels from the general public through to government and legislation.

We strive to achieve our mission through five key objectives:

1　To champion and promote fundraising
2　To set standards and promote best practice in fundraising
3　To develop and increase the individual and organisational membership
4　To support, develop and nurture the effectiveness of all fundraisers
5　To initiate, research, develop and promote new fundraising products and techniques

Key activities

- A Code of Conduct for fundraisers by which all Institute of Fundraising members must abide and support.
- Codes of Fundraising Practice for different areas of fundraising activity.
- A focal point for policy development and informing both the public and government.
- A comprehensive range of training courses for all levels.
- A competence-based professional accreditation programme.
- Regular meetings of national and regional groups.
- Regular meetings of special interest groups.
- National Convention – a three-day, intensive, practical event that provides a major focus for fundraising activity in the UK.

Training

As part of the Institute's mission, the training department seeks to support and develop the competence, effectiveness and professionalism of all those involved in fundraising.

The Certificate in Fundraising Management
The Institute launched the Certificate in Fundraising Management to give fundraisers the opportunity to undertake a professional qualification based on their fundraising competence. The Certificate has rapidly become the benchmark qualification for professional fundraisers and today over 870 fundraisers are full certificated members of the Institute of Fundraising.

The Fundraising Programme
The Institute works with members and other partners to offer over 1,000 days of fundraising training per year with over 30 titles and four levels of attainment. The Fundraising Programme is a joint venture between the Institute and the Directory of Social Change and offers a full public programme of fundraising training aimed at those who are new to fundraising through to those that manage the fundraising function.

Careerbank
The Institute of Fundraising is committed to developing, promoting and championing excellence in fundraising. As part of this mission, Careerbank supports fundraisers through their ongoing professional development. Careerbank contains a theoretical framework and a personal development record where fundraisers can chart and record their progress.

For further information please contact training@institute-of-fundraising.org.uk

Membership information

The Institute has two types of membership. Individual membership helps fundraisers become more effective in their roles. Organisational membership demonstrates an organisation's support of and commitment to the fundraising sector and environment.

Individual membership benefits include:

Professional support and networking
- Best practice from the Codes of Fundraising Practice
- Discounted access to local and technique specific support from a network of national, regional and special interest groups
- *Who's Who in Fundraising* directory

Information and services
- Online information service allowing you to choose the information you want to receive
- Free subscription to Third Sector magazine
- A legal helpline
- Discounts on a range of fundraising publications
- Access to information from the Association of Fundraising Professionals in the USA

Career development
- The Certificate in Fundraising Management
- Discounts on a range of training courses

For further information please contact membership@institute-of-fundraising.org.uk

How to contact us

Institute of Fundraising
Market Towers
1 Nine Elms Lane
London
SW8 5NQ
Telephone: 020 7627 3436
Fax: 020 7627 3508
Email: enquiries@institute-of-fundraising.org.uk
Website: www.institute-of-fundraising.org.uk

Code of Conduct

All categories of membership of the Institute are required, as a condition of their membership, to conform to the following Code of Conduct in every aspect of their professional life.

It is the duty of all members to assist the Institute in implementing and enforcing the code, and they will be supported by the Institute for so doing. Violation of the Code may lead to disciplinary action including expulsion from the Institute.

Professional conduct

All members of the Institute of Fundraising undertake to:
- conduct themselves at all times with complete integrity, honesty and trustfulness
- respect the dignity of their profession and ensure that their actions enhance the reputation of themselves and the Institute
- act according to the highest standards and visions of their organisation, profession and conscience
- advocate within their organisations adherence to all applicable laws and regulations
- avoid even the appearance of any criminal offence or professional misconduct
- bring credit to the fundraising profession by their public demeanour
- encourage colleagues to embrace and practise this Code of Conduct

They shall:
- not misuse their authority or office for personal gain
- comply with the laws of the United Kingdom which relate to their professional activities, both in letter and spirit
- advocate within their organisations compliance with the laws of the United Kingdom which relate to their professional activities, both in letter and spirit
- not exploit any relationship with a donor, prospect, volunteer or employee for personal benefit
- not knowingly, recklessly or maliciously injure the professional reputation or practice of other members of this profession
- at all times act honestly and in such a manner that donors are not misled;
- not knowingly or recklessly disseminate false or misleading information in the course of their professional duties, nor permit their subordinates to do so
- not represent conflicting or competing interests without consent of the parties concerned after full disclosure of the facts
- not knowingly act in a manner inconsistent with this Code, or knowingly cause or permit others to do so

Professional competence

All members of the Institute are expected to:
- strive to attain and apply a high level of competence to the efficient conduct of the work entrusted to them
- improve their professional knowledge and skills in order that their performance will better serve others
- recognise their individual boundaries of competence and be forthcoming and truthful about their professional experience and qualifications
- seek to ensure that all who work with them have appropriate levels of competence for the effective discharge of their duties
- endeavour always to work in harmony with their colleagues and to encourage less experienced colleagues to attain and apply their own levels of acceptable professional competence

Fundraising competence

Full and Certificated members are required to show competence in:
- establishing and communicating a case for support
- planning, organising and monitoring the allocation of resources
- research, analysis and strategy development
- coping with change and problem solving
- ability to work with colleagues, suppliers and others to achieve fundraising objectives.

Confidentiality

Members shall:
- not disclose (except as may be required by statute or law) or make use of information given or obtained in confidence from their employers or clients, the donating public or any other source without prior express consent
- adhere to the principle that all information created by, or on behalf of, an organisation is the property of an organisation and shall not be transferred or utilised except on behalf of that organisation

Donor's Charter

Members will promote and support the principles of the Donor's Charter during the course of their professional activities.

Codes of Fundraising Practice

The Codes of Fundraising Practice represent the standards set for fundraisers in the UK. Each Code covers a separate fundraising technique and provides not only information on areas of the law and guidance on the techniques themselves but also the best practice that the fundraising sector has set itself to ensure the highest standards.

Voluntary and community organisations have a duty of care to ensure that the trust invested in and confidence given to the voluntary and community sector by central and local government, police authorities, community advice bodies and most importantly, the public, is maintained. The Institute believes that developing and encouraging standards in fundraising is the key to achieving this, removing barriers to allow the sector to build healthy and productive partnerships. The Institute would urge all voluntary and community organisations that fundraise to adopt these Codes and commit to the standards within them.

The Codes are also relevant for an audience beyond practitioner fundraisers. Anyone involved in regulating or advising on fundraising, who is concerned about maintaining high standards of fundraising or who needs to know what the voluntary and community sector expects of a fundraising organisation should be aware of the Codes and demand the standards set out within them.

Currently there are Codes on the following areas:

- acceptance and refusal of donations
- charities working with business
- charity challenge events
- data protection
- fundraising from grantmaking trusts
- fundraising in schools
- fundraising on the internet
- handling cash donations
- house to house collections
- legacy fundraising
- management of static collection boxes
- outdoor fundraising events in the UK
- payment of fundraisers on a commission basis
- payroll giving
- personal solicitation for committed gifts
- raffles and lotteries
- reciprocal charity mailings
- Scottish charity law in relation to fundraising and public charitable collections in Scotland
- telephone fundraising
- telephone recruitment of collectors
- use of chain letters as a fundraising technique.

The Donor's Charter

The Donor's Charter is a statement of principle setting out a fundraiser's commitment to donors. It states the standards a donor can expect from fundraisers and organisations before, during and after the processing of the gift, be it a spontaneous donation of loose change or a substantial sum committed over many years. It also sets out the complaints procedure.

ⓘ *Further information from www.institute-of-fundraising.org.uk*

Directory

Useful organisations

Association of Charitable Foundations
Supports grantmaking trusts and foundations
2 Plough Yard
Shoreditch High Street
London
EC2A 3LP
T 020 7255 4496
www.acf.org.uk
acf@acf.org.uk

Association of Charity Officers
National umbrella body for benevolent charities, providing support for individuals in need
Unicorn House
Station Close
Potters Bar, Hertfordshire
EN6 3JW
T 01707 65177
F 01707 660477
www.aco.uk.net
info@aco.uk.net

Association of Charity Shops
Member organisation which supports charities who run shops as part of their fundraising activities
224 Shoreditch High Street
London
E1 6PJ
T 020 7422 8620
F 020 7422 8624
www.charityshops.org.uk
mail@charityshops.org.uk

Association of Chief Executives of Voluntary Organisations (ACEVO)
Professional organisation for chief executives of voluntary organisations
83 Victoria Street
London
SW1H 0HW
T 0845 345 8481
F 0845 345 8482
www.acevo.org.uk
info@acevo.org.uk

Association of Directors of Social Services
Represents directors of social services in England, Wales and Northern Ireland
Local Government House
Smith Square
London
SW1P 3HZ
T 020 7072 7433
F 020 7863 9133
www.adss.org.uk
team@adss.org.uk

Association of Fundraising Consultants
Organisation for fundraising consultants. Participates in the International Certified Fund Raising Executive qualification
enquiries@afc.org.uk

Association of Payroll Giving Agencies
Association of the main agency charities registered with the Inland Revenue to administer payroll giving on behalf of employers and members
C/o Bill Lane
South West Charitable Giving
Churchtown
Tavistock
Devon
PL19 9NP
T 01822 810094
blane@swcg.co.uk

Big Lottery Fund
New lottery fund formed from merger of lottery distributors, the Community Fund and New Opportunities Fund
1 Plough Place
London
EC4A 1DE
T 020 7211 1800
F 020 7211 1750
www.biglotteryfund.org.uk
general.enquiries@biglotteryfund.org.uk

British Association of Social Workers

Association representing social work and social workers in the UK
16 Kent Street
Birmingham
B5 6RD
T 0121 622 3911
F 0121 622 4860
www.basw.co.uk
info@basw.co.uk

Business Community Connections

Group helping charities obtain more support from business
Gainsborough House
2 Sheen Road
Richmond upon Thames, Surrey
TW9 1AE
T 020 8973 2390
F 020 8973 2396
www.bcconnections.org.uk
info@bcconnections.org.uk

Charities Aid Foundation (CAF)

International non-governmental organisation providing specialist financial services to charities and their supporters
Kings Hill
West Malling
Kent
ME19 4TA
T 01732 520000
F 01732 520001
www.cafonline.org
enquiries@CAFonline.org

Charity Commission

The regulator for charities in England and Wales
Harmsworth House
13 Bouverie Street
London
EC4Y 8DP
T 0870 333 0123
F 020 7674 2300
www.charity-commission.gov.uk
inquiries@charitycommission.gsi
.gov.uk

Charity Finance Directors' Group (CFDG)

Specialises in helping charities to manage their accounting, taxation, audit and other finance related functions
Camelford House
87–89 Albert Embankment
London
SE1 7TP
T 020 7793 1400
F 020 7793 1600
www.cfdg.org.uk
info@cfdg.org.uk

Charity Law Association

Association for those involved in or users of charity law
Roundtree Wharf
Navigation Road
York
YO1 9WE
T 01904 625790
www.charitylawassociation.org.uk
charitylaw@aol.com

Charity Trustee Networks

Sets up and provides support to networks of charity trustees
PO Box 633
Godalming
GU8 5ZX
T 01428 682252
F 01428 682252
www.trusteenetworks.org.uk
info@trusteenetworks.org.uk

Chartered Institute of Management

Organisation to support managers
2 Savoy Court
Strand
London
WC2R 0EZ
T 020 7497 0580
F 020 7497 0463
www.managers.org.uk
enquiries@managers.org.u

Chartered Institute of Marketing

The official body that sets the standards for sales and marketing professional development nationwide. Offers courses and a diploma in fundraising
Moor Hall
Cookham
Maidenhead, Berkshire
SL6 9QH
T 01628 427500
F 01628 427499
www.cim.co.uk
membership@cim.co.uk

Chartered Institute of Personnel & Development

Professional body for development of managers
CIPD House
35 Camp Road
Wimbledon, London
SW19 4UX
T 020 8971 9000
F 020 8263 3333
www.cipd.co.uk
cipd@cipd.co.uk

Commission for Racial Equality (CRE)

Publicly funded, non-governmental body set up under the Race Relations Act 1976 to tackle racial discrimination and promote racial equality
St Dunstan's House
201–211 Borough High Street
London
SE1 1GZ
T 020 7939 0000
F 020 7939 0001
www.cre.gov.uk
info@cre.gov.uk

Community Foundation Network

National network linking over 60 community foundations throughout England, Northern Ireland, Scotland and Wales
Arena House
66–68 Pentonville Road
London
N1 9HS
T 020 7713 9326
F 020 7713 9327
www.communityfoundations.
org.uk
network@communityfoundations.
org.uk

Community Service Volunteers (CSV)

Organisation promoting volunteering and training for volunteering
237 Pentonville Road
London
N1 9NJ
T 020 7278 6601
www.csv.org.uk
information@csv.org.uk

Council of Ethnic Minority Voluntary Sector Organisations (CEMVO)

Organisation promoting ethnic minority projects and urban renewal
Boardman House
64 Broadway
London
E15 1NG
T 020 8432 0307
F 020 8432 0318/9
www.enthnicminorityfund.org.uk
enquiries@emf-cemvo.co.uk

Direct Marketing Association

Trade association for the marketing and communications sector
70 Margaret Street
London
W1W 8SS
T 020 7291 3300
F 020 7323 4165
www.dma.org.uk
membership@dma.org.uk

Directory of Social Change

Independent source of information, training and support to voluntary and community sectors
24 Stephenson Way
London
NW1 2DP
T 08450 77 77 07
F 020 7391 4808
www.dsc.org.uk
info@dsc.org.uk

Disability Rights Commission (DRC)

Independent body established in April 2000 by Act of Parliament to stop discrimination and promote equality of opportunity for disabled people. Runs a helpline and conciliation service
DRC Helpline
FREEPOST MID02164
Stratford upon Avon
CV37 9BR
T 08457 622 633
F 08457 778 878
www.drc-gb.org

Equal Opportunities Commission (EOC)

Equal Opportunities Commission is an independent, non-departmental public body that deals with sex discrimination. Provides a helpline, information and publications about equality in the workplace
36 Broadway
London
SW1H 0BH
T 020 7222 1110
F 020 7222 2810
www.eoc.org.uk
info@eoc.org.uk

European Association for Planned Giving

European source of information on planned giving
Paramount House
162-170 Wardour Street
London
W1V 4AB
T 020 7734 0777
F 01622 850771
www.plannedgiving.co.uk
info@plannedgiving.org.uk

European Fundraising Association

Cross-European fundraising support group
Royal Oak House
78 Back Hill
Ely, Cambridgeshire
CB7 4B7
www.efa-net.org
efahonsec@aol.com

ICSA Charity Secretaries Group

Professional body for chartered secretaries
16 Park Crescent
London
W1B 1AH
T 020 7612 7040
F 020 7323 1132
www.icsa.org.uk
info@icsa.co.uk

Inland Revenue

Government department with responsibility for tax effective giving including Gift Aid and payroll giving
St Johns House
Merton Road
Bootle, Merseyside
L69 9BB
T 0845 302020
F 0151 472 6268/6060
www.inlandrevenue.gov.uk
charities@inlandrevenue.gov.uk

Institute of Development Professionals in Education

Professional body for all those responsible for securing additional funding and support in the education sector
Suite 33
10 Barley Mow Passage
London
W4 4PH
T 01204 880453
F 01204 880453
www.idpe.org.uk
info@idpe.org.uk

Institute of Direct Marketing

Provides membership, training, qualifications and information for marketing professionals. Runs a variety of courses including a diploma
1 Park Road
Teddington, Middlesex
TW11 0AR
T 020 8614 0277
F 020 8943 2535
www.theidm.co.uk
enquiries@theidm.com

Institute of Directors

Represents directors of businesses from large public companies to small private firms
116 Pall Mall
London
SW1Y 5ED
T 020 7839 1233
F 020 7766 8833
www.iod.com
enquiries@iod.com

Institute of Fundraising

Professional body for fundraisers. Activities include producing codes of fundraising good practice, a professional accreditation programme, annual convention and networking opportunities through special interest groups. See About the Institute section
Market Towers
1 Nine Elms Lane
London
SW8 5NQ
T 020 7627 3436
F 020 7627 3508
www.institute-of-fundraising.org.uk
info@institute-of-fundraising.org.uk

Institute of Philanthropy

Promotes research into the incentives and barriers to giving
2 Temple Place
London
WC2R 3BD
T 020 7240 0262
F 020 7240 8022
www.instituteforphilanthropy.org.uk
instituteforphilanthropy@
btinternet.com

Institute of Public Relations

Provides education and training to PR professionals
The Old Trading House
15 Northburgh Street
London
EX1V 0PR
T 020 7253 5151
F 020 7490 0588
www.ipr.org.uk
info@ipr.org.uk

Legacy Promotion Campaign

Consortium of over 120 UK charities, formed and run through the Institute of Fundraising and established to address the gap in the fundraising sector around legacies
5th Floor, Market Towers
1 Nine Elms Lane
London
SW8 5NQ
T 020 7930 2620
F 020 7627 3508
www.legacypromotioncampaign.
org.uk
theresa@institute-of-
fundraising.org.uk

Museums Association

Representative body for museums and galleries in Britain. Offers professional development, events and publications for professionals working in this sector
24 Calvin Street
London
E1 6NW
T 020 7426 6970
F 020 7426 6961
www.museumsassociation.org
info@museumsassociation.org

nfpSynergy

A think tank specialising in ideas and information about the voluntary and community sector, including research into charitable giving
70 Cowcross Street
London
EC1M 6EJ
T 020 7250 3343
F 020 7251 8138
www.nfpsynergy.net
alexandra.denye@nfpsynergy.net

National Association of Citizens Advice Bureaux

Service offering free, confidential, impartial and independent advice on issues such as debt and employment
Myddelton House
115–123 Pentonville Road
London
N1 9LZ
T 020 7833 2181
www.nacab.org.uk

National Association of Councils for Voluntary Service

Network of over 300 Councils for Voluntary Service (CVS) throughout England
Arundel Court
177 Arundel Street
Sheffield
S1 2NU
T 0114 278 6636
F 0114 278 7025
www.nacvs.org.uk
nacvs@nacvs.org.uk

National Campaign for the Arts

Independent lobbying organisation that represents all the arts. The campaign is funded entirely by its members to ensure its independence
Pegasus House
37–43 Sackville Street
London
W1S 3EH
T 020 7333 0375
F 020 7333 0660
www.artscampaign.org.uk
nca@artscampaign.org.uk

National Council for Voluntary Organisations (NCVO)

Works with and for the voluntary sector in England by providing information, advice and support and by representing the views of the sector to government and policy-makers
Regent's Wharf
8 All Saints Street
London
N1 9RL
T 020 7713 6300
F 020 7713 6300
www.ncvo-vol.org.uk
ncvo@ncvo-vol.org.uk

National Council for Work Experience

The NCWE promotes, supports and develops quality work experience for students and organisations
Prospects House
Booth Street East
Manchester
M13 9EP
T/F 0845 6015510
www.work-experience.org
workexperience@prospects.ac
.uk

Northern Ireland Council for Voluntary Action (NICVA)

Umbrella body for voluntary, community and charitable groups in Northern Ireland
61 Duncairn Gardens
Belfast, N Ireland
BT15 2GB
T 028 9087 7777
F 028 9087 7799
www.nicva.org
info@nicva.org

Public Fundraising Regulatory Association (PFRA)

Voluntary self-regulatory body for organisations involved in fundraising by direct debit on the street and door-to-door
5–11 Lavington Street
London
SE1 0N7
T 020 7401 8452
F 020 7928 2925
www.pfra.org.uk
pfra@institute-of-
fundraising.org.uk

Resource Alliance

International network working to build the capacity of not-for-profit organisations to mobilise funds and local resources for their causes
295 Kennington Road
London
SE11 4QE
T 020 75870287
F 020 7582 4335
www.resource-alliance.org
contact@resource-alliance.org

Scottish Council for Voluntary Organisations (SCVO)

Umbrella organisation for voluntary groups in Scotland
The Mansfield Traquair Centre,
15 Mansfield Place
Edinburgh
EH3 6BB
T 0131 556 3882
F 0131 556 0279
www.scvo.org.uk
enquiries@scvo.org.uk

The Media Trust

Provides communications seminars and surgeries, tailored media training, video and television production, the Community Channel and volunteering opportunities for media professionals
3–7 Euston Centre
Regent's Place
London
NW1 3JG
T 020 7874 7600
F 020 7874 7644
www.mediatrust.co.uk
info@mediatrust.org

UCAS

The university and colleges admissions service. Maintains a full list of academic institutions in the UK
Rosehill
New Barn Lane
Cheltenham, Gloucestershire
GL52 3LZ
T 01242 222444
F 01242 544960
www.ucas.com
ucas.feedback@ucas.ac.uk

UK Universities

Represents UK universities and promotes better funding in the higher education sector
Woburn House
20 Tavistock Square
London
WC1H 9HQ
T 020 7419 4111
F 020 7388 8649
www.universitiesuk.ac.uk
info@universitiesuk.ac.uk

Volunteering England

National volunteer development agency for England which came into operation on 1 April 2004. The agency brings together the Consortium on Opportunities for Volunteering, the National Centre for Volunteering and Volunteer Development England
Regent's Wharf
8 All Saints Street
London
N1 9RL
T 0845 305 6979
F 020 7520 8910
www.volunteering.org.uk
information@volunteeringengland.org

Wales Council for Voluntary Action

Represents and campaigns for voluntary organisations, volunteers and communities in Wales
Baltic House
Mount Stuart Square
Cardiff
CF10 5FH
T 0870 607 1666
F 029 2043 1701
www.wcva.org.uk
enquiries@wcva.org.uk

Online resources

fundraising.co.uk

The home of UK Fundraising, founded in 1994 to provide fundraising news, events and publications information, discussion forums and jobs

society.guardian.co.uk

Provides breaking news, analysis, comment and special reports on the voluntary sector and public services. Covers charities and voluntary organisations, health, housing, local government, regeneration and social care. Also carries information from the weekly Guardian Society supplement and offers daily and weekly email briefings
See p116 for more on Guardian Unlimited

allaboutgiving.org

Set up by the Charities Aid Foundation (CAF), All about giving is a source of information on tax-effective giving on the Internet. Users can buy charity gift vouchers, find out about giving, make donations, manage their CAF charity account online and get charity news

---

artsprofessional.co.uk
General site for those involved in management in the arts, offering information and jobs

governmentfunding.org.uk
A site managed by the Directory of Social Change and supported by the Home Office which offers a portal to grants for the voluntary and community sector from the department for education and skills, department of health, the home office, the office of the deputy Prime Minister and the government offices for the regions

guidestar.org.uk
Independent charity established in 2003 to promote the UK's voluntary and community sector. The site provides free access to a database of information on UK charities. The search facility enables users to track down charities or lists of charities by type of work, targeted beneficiaries, location or size

smartchange.org
Develops community involvement websites for companies by linking intranets to a database of UK charities. Employees are encouraged to support charities through company payroll giving and are able to access charity information on fundraising, projects, events and volunteering

thesite.org.uk
Produced and managed by YouthNet UK, a registered charity founded in 1995. Offers volunteering opportunities and information

volresource.org.uk
Practical information for people involved in charities, voluntary or community organisations. Resources include news, events, IT information and links to service providers

---

Recruitment consultants and headhunters

Action Planning
Mid-Day Court
30 Brighton Road
Sutton, Surrey
SM2 5BN
T 020 864 41122
F 020 8770 2090
www.actionplanning.co.uk
tbailey@actionplanning.co.uk
Specialises in chief executive and other senior staff appointments, particularly in fundraising, marketing and communications

Aquilas
46 Culver Road
St Albans, Hertfordshire
AL1 4ED
T 01727 375361
F 01727 834052
www.aquilas.co.uk
info@aquilas.co.uk
Specialist recruitment consultancy supplying fundraising staff solely to the charity and not-for-profit sector

Blackadders Search & Selection
30 Whitehall Street
Dundee, Scotland
DD1 4AF
T 01382 342270
F 01382 225972
www.blackadders.co.uk
searchandselection@
blackadders.co.uk
Recruitment in the not-for-profit sector

CF Appointments
Lloyds Court
1 Goodman's Yard
London
E1 8AT
T 020 79531190
F 020 7953 1191
www.cfappointments.org.uk
enquiries@CfAppointments.com
Long established consultancy specialising in the recruitment of senior executives for the charity and non-profit sector

Charity Action Recruitment
207 Waterloo Road
London
SE1 8XD
T 020 7928 2843
F 020 7633 9105
www.c-a-r.org.uk
car@lwts.org.uk

Places people in permanent, contract and temporary vacancies with charities

Charity Connections
15 Theed Street
London
SE1 8ST
T 020 7202 9000
F 020 7202 9009
www.charityconnections.co.uk
info@charityconnections.com
Executive appointments, temporary assignments, contract, interim and permanent recruitment within the charity, education, housing and arts sectors

Charity People
38 Bedford Place
London
WC1B 5JH
T 020 72998700
F 020 7636 3331
www.charitypeople.co.uk
candidates@charitypeople.co.uk
Recruitment agency for permanent, temporary and contract positions in the not-for-profit sector. Recruits at all levels across charities, housing associations and the arts . Also organises the annual Forum3 recruitment and volunteering fair (www.forum3.co.uk) supported by The Guardian and SocietyGuardian.co.uk

CR Search and Selection
40 Rosebery Avenue
London
EC1R 4RX
T 020 7833 0770
F 020 7833 0188
www.charityrecruitment.co.uk
enquiries@charityrecruit.com
Recruits at all levels in a range of
disciplines including international
aid, arts, environment, health &
welfare organisations, schools,
colleges and hospices

Eden Brown Recruitment
17–29 Sun Street
London
EC2M 2PT
T 020 7309 1300
F 020 7309 1313
www.edenbrown.co.uk
charities@edenbrown.com
Recruits across charities, arts
organisations, NGOs and academic
institutions

Execucare
34 Ebury Street
London
SW1W 0LU
T 020 7761 0700
F 020 7761 0707
www.execucare.com
info@execucare.com
Search and selection consultancy
specialising in the not-for-profit
sector, including arts, charities and
education jobs

Harris Hill
37 Market Place
Kingston Upon Thames, Surrey
KT1 1JQ
T 020 8974 9990
F 020 8974 6000
www.harrishill.co.uk
info@harrishill.co.uk
Charity and not-for-profit
recruitment specialist offering
permanent, contract and
temporary vacancies

Kingston Smith Executive Selection
Quadrant House
80–82 Regent Street
London
W1B 5RP
T 020 7306 5658
F 020 7306 5682
www.kingstonsmith.co.uk
Selection agency for chief executive
and management roles in the
voluntary sector

Oxford Human Resource Consultants Ltd
69 Observatory Street
Oxford
OX2 6EP
T 01865 510980
www.oxfordhr.co.uk
mwills@oxfordhr.co.uk
Executive search and selection
consultants serving the
international development sector

Principle Partnership
156 Tooley Street
London
SE1 2TZ
T 020 7940 4150
F 020 7940 4152
www.tpp.co.uk
fundraising@tpp.co.uk
Offers temporary, contract and
permanent positions in charities
and voluntary organisations

ProspectUs
20–22 Stukeley Street
London
WC2B 5LR
T 020 7691 1925
F 020 7691 1930
www.prospect-us.co.uk
enquiries@prospect-us.co.uk
Recruitment for charities,
universities, membership
organisations and NHS trusts in
London

Sycal Management and Recruitment
6 Northernhay Place
Exeter, Devon
EX4 5QJ
T 01392 254978
F 01392 256556
www.sycal.org.uk
recruitment@sycal.org.uk
Specialises in senior, fundraising
and marketing appointments in
not-for-profit sector

The Davis Company
First Floor
45–49 Mortimer St.
London
W1N 8JL
T 020 7323 6696
F 020 7323 6697
www.daviscompany.co.uk
Marketing and media specialist

The Kage Partnership
Linton House
164–180 Union Street
London
SE1 0LH
T 020 79283434
F 020 79289825
www.kagep.com
info@kagep.com
Specialises in fundraising,
marketing and communications
appointments in the not-for-profit
sector in and around London.

Wootton George Consulting
Pool Cottage
Radmore Lane
Cotonwood, Gnosall,
Staffordshire
ST20 0EG
T 01785 663600
F 01785 824770
www.wootton-george.co.uk
simon@wootton-george.co.uk
Places experienced fundraisers with
charities and voluntary
organisations looking for interim
managers

Xchangeteam
20/22 Stukeley Street
London
WC2B 5LR
T 020 7025 4400
F 020 7025 4401
www.xchangeteam.com
info@xchangeteam.com
Places freelance marketing and
communications professionals,
including those working in
fundraising and direct marketing

Job vacancy websites

Artshub
artshub.co.uk
UK arts sector website from original Australian version with section on fundraising jobs. Provides jobs, news, information and events. Requires paid registration

Charity Careers
charitycareers.co.uk
Job site where you can register your CV and also register for an email bulletin service. Offers bespoke services such as psychometric testing and five year action plans

CharityJOB
Charityjob.co.uk
Provides a selection of charity jobs from different recruitment consultants

Charityopps
charityopps.com
Sponsored by recruitment agency Charity Recruitment, provides a listing of jobs in the voluntary sector at all levels, with a dedicated fundraising section. Users can register their CV

Doctorjob
doctorjob.com
Graduate careers website including information about jobs in charities and fundraising, careers advice and job vacancies

Guardian Jobs
jobs.guardian.co.uk/fundraising
Jobs site from the Guardian newspaper, includes jobmatch service where you register your profile with the site and links to relevant Guardian editorial. Also includes careers advice and jobhunt tips

Jobs.ac.uk
jobs.ac.uk
Jobs listings, including fundraising posts, at UK universities. Also includes vacancies for public sector, commercial and health organisations, research institutions, charities, colleges and schools

Jobsincharities
jobsincharities.co.uk
Jobs listings for all levels of fundraising jobs – and volunteer positions

Museumjobs
museumjobs.com/uk/
Recruitment site specialising in jobs in the museum sector, including fundraising positions

Opportunities
opportunities.co.uk
Public sector recruitment site. Provides information about local authorities and the public sector, including local authority website directory

Prospects
prospects.ac.uk
Graduate recruitment site, which occasionally has fundraising vacancies and information plus graduate information

UK fundraising
fundraising.co.uk
Fundraising news and information plus jobs and training course section

Voluntarysectorjobs
voluntarysectorjobs.co.uk
General voluntary sector recruitment site which includes jobs for fundraisers

Training providers

=MC (The Management Centre)
Works with not-for-profit organisations worldwide, running management and fundraising training programmes. Runs three public fundraising training programmes: the National Arts Fundraising School, securing business sponsorship and influencing skills for fundraisers
Blue Jay Works
117 Gauden Road
London
SW4 6LE
T 020 7978 1516
F 020 7978 2125
www.managementcentre.co.uk

3rd Solutions
Collective of independent consultants and service providers, offering training, mentoring and other support for the not-for-profit sector
PO Box 138
Oswestry
SY22 6WA
T 0845 458 8236
F 0845 458 5951
www.3rdSolutions.com
enquiries@3rdsolutions.com

ADEPT Community Development Agency
Supports community involvement and capacity building projects through fundraising training and consultancy
3 Market Way
Coventry
CV1 1DF
T 024 7623 0606
www.adept.org.uk
lea@adept.org.uk

Arts Marketing Association

Professional development body for anyone involved in promoting the arts and cultural industries in the UK. Runs training and events programme
7a Clifton Court
Clifton Road
Cambridge
CB1 7BN
T 01223 578078
F 01223 578079
www.a-m-a.co.uk
info@a-m-a.co.uk

The Association of Fundraising Consultants

Offers a UK version of the Certified Fund Raising Executive (CFRE), an international credential for senior professional fundraisers
PO Box 9
Woodstock
OX20 1ZJ
T 01582 762446
F 01582 461489
www.afc.org.uk
enquiries@afc.org.uk

Brakeley Ltd

Fundraising consultancy offering training in basic fundraising and executive coaching
Paramount House
162–170 Wardour Sreet
London
W1V 4AB
T 020 72873361
F 020 72878705
www.brakeley.com
info@brakeley.com

Cass Business School, City of London

Offers a postgraduate diploma and masters in charity marketing and fundraising. Completion of diploma leads to the Institute of Fundraising's Certificate in Fundraising Management
106 Bunhill Row
London
EC1Y 8TZ
T 020 7040 8600
F 020 7040 5060
www.cass.city.ac.uk
g.m.harris@city.ac.uk

Charities Advisory Trust

Offers graduate training schemes including placements in the voluntary sector
Radius Works
Back Lane
London
NW3 1HL
T 020 7794 9835
F 020 7431 3739
www.charitiesadvisorytrust.co.uk
people@charitiesadvisorytrust
.co.uk

Charities Aid Foundation (CAF)

CAF organises a wide variety of conferences, seminars and workshops for the non-profit sector and its supporters, in key areas such as funding and tax-effective giving
114–118 Southampton Row
London
WC1B 5AA
T 020 7400 2300
F 020 7831 0134
www.cafonline.org
enquiries@CAFonline.org

Charities Information Bureau

Training and information organisation with expertise in funding and funding related matters for the community and voluntary sector
93 Lawfield Lane
Wakefield, West Yorkshire
WF2 8SU
T 01924 239063
F 01924 239431
www.cibfunding.org.uk
funding@the-cib.demon.co.uk

Charity Consultants Ltd

Offer in-house training courses for small groups (from six staff, or two or more charities) who want to get together for training
Little Holme
Station Road
Shiplake, Henley on Thames
RG9 3JS
T 0118 940 1016
www.charityconsultants.co.uk

Company Solutions

Training agency for the not-for-profit sector. Runs fundraising courses and masterclasses covering range of subjects, including trusts, legacies and direct marketing
Farplace
Sidehead, Westgate
Co Durham
DL13 1LE
T 01388 517703
F 01388 517044
www.companysolutions.biz
gareth@companysolutions.biz

Directory of Social Change

Runs the Fundraising Programme with the Institute of Fundraising, a four-level training programme for fundraisers in large and small organisations. Advanced courses lead to the Institute of Fundraising's Certificate in Fundraising Management
24 Stephenson Way
London
NW1 2DP
T 08450 77 77 07
F 020 7391 4808
www.dsc.org.uk/charitytraining
thefundraisingprogramme@
dsc.org.uk

Environmental Trainers Network

Established in 1991 as a network of trainers and training managers in environmental organisations, and overseen by a steering group drawn from Black Environment Network, BTCV, Groundwork, RSPB and the Wildlife Trust
c/o BTCV
47–50 Hockley Hill, Hockley
Birmingham
B18 5AQ
T 0121 507 8390
F 0121 507 8391
www.btcv.org/etn
ETN@unite.net

Fresh Fields

Provides training for people who want to work in the voluntary sector. Runs a two-day weekend residential course covering sector history and trends, fundraising methods and job-hunting advice
The Little House
Bath Road, Norton St Philip
Bath
BA3 6LP
T 01373 834497

Fundraising Training Limited

Runs the fast track Fundraising Trainee Programme and advanced training courses in strategic planning, financial skills and building relationships with funders
PO Box 240
Wallingford
OX10 9XZ
T 01491 202070
F 01491 202070
www.frtr.co.uk
bill@frtr.co.uk

Fundraising UK

Offers bespoke training in internet fundraising, including use of email as a fundraising technique and how to use the internet for funding research
17 Errington Road
Colchester, Essex
CO3 3EA
T 01206 579081
www.fundraising.co.uk
hlake@fundraising.co.uk

Holmes Consultancy Services

Training courses for fundraisers and charity managers
9 Lilford Close
Glebe Park
Lincoln
LN2 4TG
T 01522 544927
F 01522 527255
www.hcsuk.com
info@hcsuk.com

Institute of Fundraising

Offers Certificate in Fundraising Management, a vocational qualification for fundraisers based on competencies. Also offers Careerbank professional development service for members and bespoke training for charities. The Institute's special interest groups and regional groups also arrange events for fundraisers
Market Towers
1 Nine Elms Lane
London
SW8 5NQ
T 020 7627 2806
F 020 7627 3508
www.institute-of-fundraising.org.uk
training@institute-of-fundraising.org.uk

Institute of Legacy Management

Offers the ILM Certificate of Competence, created and run in association with the College of Law. Also runs seminars and an annual meeting for legacy officers
PO Box 173, Bakewell Road
Orton Southgate, Peterborough
PE2 6WS
T 01733 375227
www.ilmnet.org
ilm@mib.org.uk

InterChange Training

Staff development service for voluntary, arts and public sector organisations
InterChange Studios
Hampstead Town Hall Centre,
213 Haverstock Hill
London
NW3 4QP
T 020 7692 5866
F 020 7813 7493
www.interchange.org.uk/training
training@interchange.org.uk

Learndirect.co.uk

Online courses in computers, office skills and self development. Information on network of over 2,000 learndirect centres
5th Floor
88 Kingsway
London
WC2B 6AA
T 0800 101 901
F 020 7681 6602
www.learndirect.co.uk
enquiries@learndirect.net

London Voluntary Sector Training Consortium

Set up by a consortium of voluntary sector training providers in 1989. Offers strategic development and training in the voluntary and community sectors
18 Ashwin Street
London
E8 3DL
T 020 7249 4441
F 020 7923 4280
www.lvstc.org.uk
info@lvstc.org.uk

London Voluntary Service Council (LVSC)

Arranges tailored in-house training and offers a range of short courses including training in fundraising strategy
356 Holloway Road
London
N7 6PA
T 020 7700 8113
F 020 7700 8108
www.lvsc.org.uk
training@lvsc.org.uk

London South Bank University – Centre for Government and Charity Management (CGCM)

Offers postgraduate certificate, diploma and MSc in voluntary sector management
London Road Business School
South Bank University
103 Borough Road
London
SE1 0AA
T 020 7815 7821
F 020 7815 6140
www.lsbu.ac.uk/bcim/business/cgcm
karhellh@lsbu.ac.uk

NACVS

Runs national training programme and circulates details of training done by local CVS (councils for voluntary service)
177 Arundel Street
Sheffield
S1 2NU
T 0114 278 6636
F 0114 278 7004
www.nacvs.org.uk
nacvs@nacvs.org.uk

Northern Ireland Council for Voluntary Action

Offers management development programme for voluntary sector managers in Northern Ireland
61 Duncairn Gardens
Belfast
BT15 2GB
T 028 9087 7777
F 028 9087 7799
www.nicva.org
sandra.bailie@nicva.org

Professional Fundraising Consultancy
Offers Certificate in Fundraising for Schools as well as fundraising courses and masterclasses
Lancaster House
Leslie Avenue
Caton, Lancashire
LA2 9RE
T 01524 770990
F 01524 770808
www.pfconsultancy.co.uk
info@pfconsultancy.co.uk

Kew Quorum
Provides mentoring for fundraisers, particularly new fundraising directors or chief executives of smaller charities with a responsibility for fundraising. Also provides customised, in house fundraising training and interim management
Weir House
Towpath
Shepperton
Middlesex
TW17 9LL
T/F 01932 224717
www.kewquorum.co.uk
peter@kewquorum.co.uk

Scottish Council for Voluntary Organisations (SCVO)
SCVO's development and programmes directorate provides learning and skills support to individuals and organisations working in the voluntary sector in Scotland
The Mansfield Traquair Centre
15 Mansfield Place
Edinburgh
EH3 6BB
T 0131 474 8017
F 0131 557 6483
www.scvo.org.uk
celia.carson@scvo.org.uk

Sheffield Hallam University
Offers the Institute of Fundraising's Certificate in Fundraising Management
City Campus
Howard Street, Sheffield
South Yorkshire
S1 1WB
T 0114 225 5231
F 0114 225 2094
www.shu.ac.uk
enquiries@shu.ac.uk

Smee and Ford
Legacy fundraising agency providing training
St George's House
195/203 Waterloo Road
London
SE1 8UX
T 020 7928 4050
F 020 7928 5837
www.smeeandford.co.uk
richard@smeeandford.co.uk

The Open University – Open University Business School
Runs the Winning resources and support course, leading to the Institute of Fundraising's Certificate in Fundraising Management (subject to membership conditions). Also offers Professional Certificate in Management – public & non-profit organisations
Walten Hall
Milton Keynes
MK7 6AA
T 01908 653454
F 01908 652247
www.open.ac.uk
general-enquiries@open.ac.uk

The Projects Company
Provides Certificate in Fundraising Management
Willow Lodge
Church Road High Beach
Loughton
Essex
IG10 4AJ
T 020 8502 2327
F 020 8502 2328
www.theprojectsco.co.uk
info@theprojectsco.co.uk

Valley Arts Marketing
Specialists in arts marketing, research and database management
Lower Park Lodge
Glan Road
Aberdare
CF44 8BN
T 01685 884247
F 01685 884249
www.v-a-m.org.uk
training@v-a-m.org.uk

Voluntary Arts Network
Provides information about training for arts professionals and links to specialist training providers
PO Box 200
Cardiff
CF5 1YH
T 02920 395 395
F 02920 397 397
www.voluntaryarts.org
info@voluntaryarts.org

Volunteering England
Volunteering England and AM Training work in partnership to offer professional level training for people who manage volunteers
Regents Wharf
8 All Saints Street
London
N1 9RL
T 0845 305 6979
F 020 7520 8910
www.volunteering.org.uk/training
information@volunteeringengland.org

Wales Council for Voluntary Action
Provides fundraising and management development training
Baltic House
Mount Stuart Square
Cardiff Bay
Cardiff
CF10 5FH
T 02920431700
F 029 20431701
www.wcva.org.uk
enquiries@wcva.org.uk

Working for a Charity
Independent organisation set up to promote the voluntary sector as a positive career option. Offers short introductory courses with placements in the voluntary sector
The Peel Centre
Percy Circus
London
WC1X 9EY
T 020 7833 8220
F 020 7833 1820
www.wfac.org.uk
enquiries@wfac.org.uk

Magazines and journals

Arts Professional
News, views, reviews and case studies for UK arts managers
PO Box 957
Cottenham, Cambridge
CB4 8AB
T 01954 250600
F 01954 252600
subs@artsprofessional.co.uk
www.artsprofessional.co.uk
Published by Arts Professional
Fortnightly

Association Manager
News and advice for the UK's associations, institutes, unions and other membership organisations.
3 Rectory Grove
London
SW4 0DX
T 020 7819 1200
F 020 7819 1219
subscriptions@association
manager.co.uk
www.associationmanager.co.uk
Published by Plaza Publishing
Ltd
Bi-monthly

Care*and*Health
News, analysis, comment and jobs for health and social care professionals
21–27 Seagrave Road
London
SW6 1RP
T 0870 901 7773
F 0870 901 7774
amanda.johnstone@
careandhealth.com
www.careandhealth.com
Published by Care*and*Health Ltd
Fortnightly

Charity Finance
Business magazine for charity sector professionals.
3 Rectory Grove
London
SW4 0DX
T 020 7819 1200
info@charityfinance.co.uk
www.charityfinance.co.uk
Published by Plaza Publishing
Ltd
Monthly

Charity Times
Business and management magazine for UK non-profit professionals.
402 The Fruit & Wool Exchange
Brushfield Street
London
E1 6EP
T 020 7426 0636
F 020 7426 0123
jon.muir@perspectivepublishing
.com
www.charitytimes.com
Published by Perspective
Publishing
Monthly

Community Care
Provides news, features, comment and analysis of social care
Quadrant House
The Quadrant Sutton
Sutton, Surrey
SM2 5AS
T 01444 475612
F 01444 445441
jill.bright@rbi.co.uk
www.community-care.co.uk
Published by Reed Business
Information Ltd
Weekly

Corporate Citizenship Briefing
News and archive of citizenship and community affairs stories for corporate social responsibility practitioners.
Ground Floor South, Cottons
Centre, London Bridge City
London
SE1 2QG
T 020 7945 6130
F 020 7945 6138
mail@corporate-citizenship.co.uk
www.ccbriefing.co.uk
Published by The Corporate
Citizenship Company
Bi-monthly

Funding for Change
Information and discussion about support for voluntary activity from all potential sources: grantmaking trusts, companies, government, and the lottery.
24 Stephenson Way
London NW1 2DP
T 08450 777707
F 020 7391 4804
info@dsc.org.uk
www.dsc.org.uk
Published by Directory of Social
Change
Quarterly

The International Journal of Nonprofit and Voluntary Sector Marketing
Articles and case studies on fundraising and marketing, written by practitioners, consultants and academics.
Russell House
28–30 Little Russell Street
London
WC1A 2HN
T 020 7404 3040
F 020 7404 2081
gweny@henrystewart.co.uk
www.henrystewart.com
Published by Henry Stewart
Publications
Quarterly

Marketing
News magazine for the marketing community
174 Hammersmith Road
London
W6 7JP
T 020 8606 7500
F 020 8267 4504
csmith@haynet.com
haymarket@wdis.co.uk
Published by Haymarket
Business Publications Ltd
Weekly

Marketing Direct

Magazine for direct marketing professionals
174 Hammersmith Road
London
W6 7JP
T 020 8606 7500
F 020 8267 4192
subscriptions@haynet.com
www.mxdirect.co.uk
Published by Haymarket
Business Publications Ltd
11 times a year

Marketing Week

News and information for marketing, advertising and media professionals
50 Poland Street
London
W1V 4AX
T 020 7292 3711
F 020 7970 6721
michael.mcauley@centaur.co.uk
www.marketing-week.co.uk
Published by Centaur
Communications
Weekly

Non-Profit-Times

Business publication for non-profit management
Suite 120
120 Littletion Road
Parsippany, New Jersey (USA)
07054-1803
T 001-973-394-1800
F 001-973-394-2888
ednchief@nptimes.com
www.nptimes.com
Published by John D. McIlquham
Monthly

PR Week

News, analysis and jobs for the public relations industry
174 Hammersmith Road
London
W6 7JP
T 020 8606 7500
F 020 8267 4509
prweek@haynet.com
www.prweekuk.com
Published by Haymarket
Business Publications Ltd
Weekly

Precision Marketing

Business magazine for direct marketing professionals working in charities, DM agencies and supplier organisations
12–26 Lexington Street
London
W1R 4HQ
T 020 7970 4000
F 020 7970 4496
precision-marketing@
centaur.co.uk
www.centaur.co.uk
Published by Centaur
Communications
Weekly

Professional Fundraising

Journal for fundraisers working in charities and voluntary organisations covering news, features and jobs. Subscribers also receive PF Plus newsletter and email update
United House
41 North Road
London
N7 9DP
T 020 7700 3479
F 020 7700 2049
info@tmdpress.com
www.professionalfundraising.
co.uk
Published by TM&D Press
Monthly

Regeneration & Renewal

Aimed at professionals involved in government-backed regeneration and community renewal projects
174 Hammersmith Road
London
W6 7JP
T 020 8606 7500
F 020 8267 4003
regeneration@haynet.com
www.regenerationmagazine.com
Published by Haymarket
Publications
Weekly

SocietyGuardian

News, analysis, comment and jobs for people working in public services and the voluntary sector. Covers charities and voluntary organisations, health, housing, local government, regeneration and social care. Its sister website (societyguardian.co.uk) includes breaking news, events information and job links
119 Farringdon Road
London
EC1R 3ER
T 020 7278 2332
F 020 7713 4154
society@guardian.co.uk
http://society.guardian.co.uk
Published by Guardian
Newspapers Limited
Weekly

The Big Issue

News & current affairs magazine written by professional journalists and sold on the streets by vendors looking to overcome the crises surrounding homelessness
1–5 Wandsworth Road
London
SW8 2LN
T 020 7526 3200
F 020 7526 3202
editorial@bigissue.com
www.bigissue.com
Published by Big Issue
Company Ltd
Weekly

TFN (Third Force News – Scotland)

National newspaper in Scotland covering the country's voluntary sector issues
SCVO
Mansfield Traquair Centre,
15 Mansfield
Edinburgh
EH3 6BB
T 0131 556 3882
F 0131 556 0279
publications@scvo.org.uk
www.scvo.org.uk
Published by Scottish Council for
Voluntary Organisations
Weekly

The Chronicle of Philanthropy
US newspaper and online resource for charity leaders, fundraisers, grant makers and other people involved in philanthropy
1255 23rd St. N.W. Suite 700
Washington, D.C. 20037
USA
T 001-202-466-1200
help@philanthropy.com
philanthropy.com
Published by The Chronicle of Philanthropy
Bi-monthly

Third Sector
News magazine for voluntary sector professionals including job vacancies and Institute of Fundraising news
174 Hammersmith Road
London
W6 7JP
T 020 8606 7500
F 020 8267 4806
ThirdSector@haynet.com
www.thirdsector.co.uk
Published by Haymarket Publications
Weekly

Voluntary Sector
Published by NCVO, provides mix of news and features about the voluntary sector plus new policy developments, the fiscal environment, ethical debates and current trends
Regent's Wharf
8 All Saints Street
London
N1 9RL
T 020 7520 2467
F 020 7713 5635
amanda.moss@ncvo-vol.org.uk
www.voluntarysector.co.uk
Published by National Council for Voluntary Organisations (NCVO)
10 times a year

Books

CharityTrends
Charities Aid Foundation & CaritasData
Paulton House
8 Shepherdess Walk
London
N1 7LB
T 020 7566 8210
eswanevelder@caritasdata.co.uk
www.charitiesdirect.com

Community Fundraising – The DSC/CAF/Institute of Fundraising Series
Directory of Social Change
24 Stephenson Way
London
NW1 2DP
T 08450 777707
F 020 7391 4804
books@dsc.org.uk
www.dsc.org.uk

Corporate Fundraising – The DSC/CAF/Institute of Fundraising Series
Directory of Social Change
24 Stephenson Way
London
NW1 2DP
T 08450 777707
F 020 7391 4804
books@dsc.org.uk
www.dsc.org.uk

Effective Fundraising
Directory of Social Change
24 Stephenson Way
London
NW1 2DP
T 08450 777707
F 020 7391 4804
books@dsc.org.uk
www.dsc.org.uk

Fundraising Databases – The DSC/CAF/Institute of Fundraising Series
Directory of Social Change
24 Stephenson Way
London
NW1 2DP
T 08450 777707
F 020 7391 4804
books@dsc.org.uk
www.dsc.org.uk

Fundraising Strategy – The DSC/CAF/Institute of Fundraising Series
Directory of Social Change
24 Stephenson Way
London
NW1 2DP
T 08450 777707
F 020 7391 4804
books@dsc.org.uk
www.dsc.org.uk

Futureskills 2003
Voluntary Sector National Training Organisation
Regent's Wharf
8 All Saint's Street
London
N1 9RL
T 020 7713 6161
F 020 7713 6300
vsnto@ncvo-vol.org.uk
www.voluntarysectorskills.org.uk

Legacy Fundraising – The DSC/CAF/Institute of Fundraising Series
Directory of Social Change
24 Stephenson Way
London
NW1 2DP
T 08450 777707
F 020 7391 4804
books@dsc.org.uk
www.dsc.org.uk

Marketing Strategy – The DSC/CAF/Institute of Fundraising Series
Directory of Social Change
24 Stephenson Way
London
NW1 2DP
T 08450 777707
F 020 7391 4804
books@dsc.org.uk
www.dsc.org.uk

School Fundraising in England
Directory of Social Change
24 Stephenson Way
London
NW1 2DP
T 08450 777707
F 020 7391 4804
books@dsc.org.uk
www.dsc.org.uk

The Complete Fundraising Handbook
Directory of Social Change and
Institute of Fundraising
24 Stephenson Way
London
NW1 2DP
T 08450 777707
F 020 7391 4804
books@dsc.org.uk
www.dsc.org.uk

Trust Fundraising – The DSC/CAF/Institute of Fundraising Series
Directory of Social Change
24 Stephenson Way
London
NW1 2DP
T 08450 777707
F 020 7391 4804
books@dsc.org.uk
www.dsc.org.uk

UK voluntary sector training courses review
Directory of Social Change
24 Stephenson Way
London
NW1 2DP
T 08450 777707
F 020 7391 4804
books@dsc.org.uk
www.dsc.org.uk

Voluntary Agencies Directory
National Council for Voluntary
Organisations
Regent's Wharf
8 All Saints Street
London
N1 9RL
T 020 7713 6161
F 020 7713 6300
helpdesk@ncvo-vol.org.uk
www.ncvo-vol.org.uk

Voluntary Sector Almanac
National Council for Voluntary
Organisations
Regent's Wharf
8 All Saints Street
London
N1 9RL
T 020 7713 6161
F 020 7713 6300
helpdesk@ncvo-vol.org.uk
www.ncvo-vol.org.uk

Who's Who in Fundraising
Institute of Fundraising
Market Towers, 1 Nine Elms Lane
London
SW8 5NQ
T 020 7627 3436
F 020 7627 3508
enquiries@institute-of-fundraising.org.uk
www.institute-of-fundraising.org.uk

Writing Better Fundraising Applications
Directory of Social Change
24 Stephenson Way
London
NW1 2DP
T 08450 777707
F 020 7391 6300
books@dsc.org.uk
www.dsc.org.uk

Events

Contact event organiser for dates

AFP International Conference on Fundraising
Association of Fundraising
Professionals
1101 King Street, Suite 700
Alexandria
VA 22314
USA
T 001-703 684 0410
F 001-703 684 050
www.afpnet.org

Annual Fundraising Conference
Directory of Social Change
24 Stephenson Way
London
NW1 2DP
T 08450 777707
F 020 7391 4808
www.dsc.org.uk
info@dsc.org.uk

Annual Payroll Conference
Institute of Payroll & Pensions
Shelly House
Farmhouse Way, Monkspath
Solihull, West Midlands
B90 4EH
T 0121 712 1073
www.ippm.org.uk
caroline.turner@ippm.org

CAF Annual Conference & Exhibition
Charities Aid Foundation
114–118 Southampton Row
London
WC1B 5AA
T 01732 520000
F 01732 520001
www.cafonline.org
events@cafonline.org

Corporates & Communities Conference
Charities Aid Foundation
114–118 Southampton Row
London
WC1B 5AA
T 01732 520000
F 01732 520001
www.ccinet.org
lisap@cafonline.org

Charity Law Conference
Directory of Social Change and
Bates, Wells Braithwaite
Solicitors
24 Stephenson Way
London
NW1 2DP
T 08450 777707
F 020 7391 4808
www.dsc.org.uk
training@dsc.org.uk

Charityfair
Directory of Social Change
24 Stephenson Way
London
NW1 2DP
T 08450 777707
F 020 7391 4808
www.dsc.org.uk
cfevents@dsc.org.uk

Charity Shops Annual Conference
The Association of Charity Shops
224 Shoreditch High Street
London
E1 6PJ
T 020 7422 8620
F 020 7422 8624
www.charityshops.org.uk
mail@charityshops.org.uk

CHASE – The Charities and Associations Exhibition
Conference House Ltd
Silver Ley, Farley Green
Stradishall
Newmarket, Suffolk
CB8 8PY
T 08707 300377
F 08707 369369
www.conferencehouse.co.uk/chase/
chase@kingstonsmith.co.uk

Forum3 – recruitment and volunteering event
Charity People
38 Bedford Street
London
WC1B 5JH
T 020 7299 8702
www.forum3.co.uk
visitorinfo@charitypeople.co.uk

Institute of Fundraising National Convention
Institute of Fundraising
Market Towers
1 Nine Elms Lane
London
SW8 5NQ
T 020 7627 3436
F 020 7627 3508
www.institute-of-fundraising.org.uk
convention@institute-of-fundraising.org.uk

Institute of Fundraising North West Annual Fundraising Conference
Institute of Fundraising North West
Market Towers
1 Nine Elms Lane
London
SW8 5NQ
T 020 7627 3436
F 020 7627 3508
northwest@institute-of-fundraising.org.uk

Institute of Fundraising Northern Ireland Annual Fundraising Convention
Institute of Fundraising Northern Ireland
Market Towers
1 Nine Elms Lane
London
SW8 5NQ
T 020 7627 3436
F 020 7627 3508
www.institute-of-fundraising.org.uk
northernireland@institute-of-fundraising.org.uk

Institute of Fundraising Scotland Annual Fundraising Conference
Institute of Fundraising Scotland
Market Towers
1 Nine Elms Lane
London
SW8 5NQ
T 020 7627 3436
F 020 7627 3508
www.institute-of-fundraising.org.uk
scotland@institute-of-fundraising.org.uk

Institute of Fundraising South West Conference
Institute of Fundraising South West
17 North Street
Norton St Philip
Bath, Somerset
BA2 7LE
T 01179441200
T 020 7627 3436
F 020 7627 3508
www.institute-of-fundraising.org.uk
southwest@institute-of-fundraising.org.uk

Institute of Fundraising Wales Annual Fundraising Conference
Institute of Fundraising Wales
14–16 Merthyr Rd
Whitchurch Cardiff
CF14 1DG
T 020 7627 3436
F 020 7627 3508
www.institute-of-fundraising.org.uk
cymru@institute-of-fundraising.org.uk

International Fundraising Congress (IFC)
Resource Alliance
295 Kennington Road
London
SE11 4QE
T 020 7587 0287
F 020 7582 4335
http://resource-alliance.org
ifc@resource-alliance.org

International Workshop on Resource Mobilisation (IWRM)
Resource Alliance
295 Kennington Road
London
SE11 4QE
T 020 7587 0287
F 020 7582 4335
http://resource-alliance.org
iwrm@resource-alliance.org

Kaleidoscope – voluntary and public sector careers fair
University of Manchester & UMIST
T 0161 275 2828
www.graduatecareersonline.com/fairs/kaleidoscope
caroline.birch@man.ac.uk

National Social Services Conference
Association of Directors of Social Services and Local Government Association
County Hall
North County Council
Northallerton, North Yorkshire
DL7 8AD
T 0160 977 0661
F 0160 077 8199
www.adss.org.uk
amanda.fry@northyorks.gov.uk

NCVO Annual Conference
NCVO
Regent's Wharf
8 All Saints Street
London
N1 9RL
T 020 7520 2446
www.ncvo-vol.org.uk
gillen.knight@ncvo-vol.org.uk

Professional Fundraising
Professional Fundraising
magazine
Omnibus House
41 North Road
London
N7 9DP
T 020 7700 3479
F 020 7700 2049
www.professionalfundraising
.co.uk

Trustee Annual Conference
NCVO
Regent's Wharf
8 All Saints Street
London
N1 9RL
T 020 7713 6161
www.ncvo-vol.org.uk
trustee.admin@ncvo-vol.org.uk

Awards

Contact awards organiser for current dates

Arts & Business Awards
Arts & Business
Nutmeg House
60 Gainsford Street
Butlers Wharf
London
SE1 2NY
T 020 7378 8143
F 020 7407 7527
www.aandb.org.uk
awards@AandB.org.uk

Beacon Fellowship Prize
The Beacon Fellowship
12 St. James's Square
London
SW1Y 4RB
T 020 7849 6550
F 020 7849 6561
www.beaconfellowship.org.uk

Charities' Online Accounts Awards
CAF – Charities Aid Foundation
and the Institute of Chartered
Accountants
114–118 Southampton Row
London
WC1B 5AA
T 020 7400 2300
F 020 7831 0134
www.cafonline.org/onlineawards/
events@cafonline.org

Charity Awards
Charity Finance
3 Rectory Grove
London
SW4 0DX
T 020 7819 1209
F 020 7819 1226
www.charityawards.co.uk
alice@charityfinance.co.uk

Community Care Awards
Community Care
11th Floor Quadrant House
The Quadrant
Sutton, Surrey
SM2 5AS
T 020 8652 8863
www.communitycare.co.uk
debra.latus@rbi.co.uk

Hollis Sponsor Awards
Hollis PR
Harlequin House
7 High Street
Teddington, Middlesex
TW11 8EL
T 020 8977 7711
F 020 8977 1133
www.hollis-pr.com

Institute of Fundraising & Professional Fundraising Awards
Institute of Fundraising and
Professional Fundraising
Magazine
United House
41 North Road
London
N7 9DP
T 020 7700 3479
F 020 7700 2049
www.institute-of-
fundraising.org.uk
www.professionalfundraising.
co.uk

North West Fundraising Awards
Institute of Fundraising North
West
Market Towers
1 Nine Elms Lane
London
SW8 5NQ
T 020 7627 3436
F 020 7627 3508
www.institute-of-
fundraising.org.uk
northwest@institute-of-
fundraising.org.uk

Scottish Fundraising Awards
Institute of Fundraising Scotland
Market Towers
1 Nine Elms Lane
London
SW8 5NQ
T 020 7627 3436
F 020 7627 3508
www.institute-of-
fundraising.org.uk
fiona.duncan@capability-
scotland.org.uk

UK Charity Awards
Charity Times
402 The Fruit & Wool Exchange
Brushfield Street
London
E1 6EP
T 020 7426 0424
F 020 7426 0042
www.charitytimes.com
jenni.williams@perspective
publishing.com

Glossary

Acquisition mailing (or prospect mailing)
A mailing to prospects to acquire new members or donors.

Affinity fundraising
A partnership between a fundraising organisation such as a charity, and a commercial organisation where the former markets or endorses the latter's service or product to its supporters or members in return for a percentage of the income gained from new or additional business. Also known as **cause-related marketing** (see below)

Appeal
A one-off or ongoing request for funds for a specific project or cause e.g. overseas disaster relief or new local hospital wing.

Beneficiary
Legal term referring to recipient groups or individuals of a charity's work, or a grantmaking body's funding, for example homeless people or children.

Big gifts/major gifts
Large donations, often given by wealthy donors or companies ('major donors'), for specific projects e.g. new building or anniversary project.

Big Lottery Fund
New lottery funds distributor formed from the merger of the Community Fund and the New Opportunities Fund and launched in June 2004. Legislation to constitute the new body as a separate legal entity is expected to complete its passage through Parliament by autumn 2005. The new distributor will continue the two funds' support for charities and the voluntary sector, health, education and the environment. It will also take on the Millennium Commission's ability to fund large-scale regeneration projects.

Capital appeal
A structured fundraising programme to raise a set target amount for a specific need and within a specific time frame.

Campaign
An organised effort to raise funds for a not-for-profit organisation.

Cause-related marketing
A commercial activity by which businesses and charities or causes form a partnership with each other to market an image, product or service for mutual benefit. *Also see* **Affinity fundraising**

Charity Commission

The body established by law as the regulator and registrar for charities in England and Wales. Produces operational guidance on charity law and practice and maintains a publicly accessible register of charities.

Charitable foundation

An organisation, usually with a specific interest such as poverty or children, that awards grants to charities for project work. Historically set up by wealthy families or individuals, charitable foundations and trusts are increasingly being used by companies as a vehicle for their corporate giving.

Charitable purpose

To register as a charity, an organisation must have purposes that are charitable. These have been defined by case law and by the Charity Commission. In addition to the original objects of advancing education and religion and relieving poverty, charitable purpose now extends to a wide range of activities including conservation of the environment, work with refugees and urban regeneration. The draft Charities Bill published in May 2004 proposes 12 charitable purposes:

- the prevention or relief of poverty
- the relief of those in need by reason of youth, old age, ill-health, disability, financial hardship or other disadvantage
- the advancement of:
  - education
  - religion
  - health
  - citizenship or community development
  - arts, heritage or science
  - amateur sport
  - animal welfare
  - human rights, conflict resolution or reconciliation
  - environmental protection or improvement

- any other purposes that are, or may be in future, recognised under charity law.

Charitable trust

See **Charitable foundation**

Charity law

Legal requirements for registered charities, many of which have been established or tested in the courts. Includes regulations on trustees, accounts and finances, campaigning and management.

Charities Bill

Published in May 2004, the draft Charities Bill is designed to overhaul 400-year-old charity law. It proposes that all registered charities will have to pass a public benefit test; 12 charitable purposes; a local authority licensing scheme for public collections, including face-to-face fundraising and 'reserve powers' for the Home Secretary to introduce fundraising regulation is needed. Announced in the Queen's speech in November 2003, the draft Bill follows the Home Office's response to the prime minister's Strategy Unit's 2002 report Private Action, Public Benefit.

Chuggers

Slang. Abbreviation for 'charity muggers', used to describe face-to-face fundraisers who approach members of the public in the street *(see* **Face-to-face fundraising***)*

Codes of Fundraising Practice

The Institute of Fundraising Codes of Fundraising Practice represent the standards set for fundraisers in the UK. In addition to the Donor's Charter, there are codes on fundraising conduct; working with business and accepting or refusing donations. A further 20 codes cover fundraising techniques.

Commercial participator
A business or individual who engages in any promotional venture resulting in contributions being given to charity (such as in cause-related marketing).

Committed giving
Regular giving by donors via methods such as direct debits, payroll giving or membership schemes.

Community foundation
Local area-based grantmaking trusts that derive their income in gifts from trusts, bequests, shares or property to create a permanent endowment. This is then used to award cash of long-term benefit to voluntary and community groups within their area, providing a sustainable flow of funds for local good causes.

Community Fund
Distributor of National Lottery money for specific projects to charities and voluntary organisations. An 'administrative merger' of the fund with the New Opportunities Fund in 2004 will eventually create a single body (*see* **Big Lottery Fund**)

Community fundraising
Area-based fundraising targeting local sources of funding such as schools, clubs, church groups etc.

Compact
An agreement between the government and the whole voluntary and community sector made in 1998 to improve their relationship for mutual advantage. The national Compact's principles have now been turned into codes of practice on funding, consultation, volunteering, community groups and BME (black and minority ethnic) groups.

Core funding
The money required for operational, management and day-to-day costs of a charity. Examples of areas covered by core funding include fundraising, administration, property costs and staff salaries. Sometimes also relates to a charity's main source of income e.g. public donations or grants.

Corporate fundraising
Soliciting donations of money, time or goods from companies. Increasingly linked to corporate social responsibility (see below) and measurable commercial benefits such as enhanced image or goodwill with customers and suppliers.

Corporate social responsibility
An approach taken by a company to meet or exceed stakeholder expectations in areas such as community investment, employee relations, environmental practices and ethical conduct.

Data Protection Act
The 1998 Data Protection Act regulates how information relating to individuals should be processed. This governs how fundraisers and others should handle a donor's personal data. The Act sets out eight data protection principles that govern how information collected should be used and protected.

Deed of covenant
An agreement between a charity and a donor for a specified sum of money to be given over a set period of time.

Direct debit
Method of transmitting money where the charity or other organisation claims a payment from the donor's bank, often on a monthly basis so providing a regular source of income for the recipient.

Direct dialogue

Directly engaging people in conversation on behalf of a charity, and encouraging them to support that charity through planned, regular giving by direct debit. Examples include street and door-to-door fundraising.

Direct mail

A postal communication mailed out to acquire new supporters or to develop existing ones. The mailing may be designed to solicit a one-off or ongoing donation, or encourage membership of the organisation.

Direct marketing

Solicitation of gifts or volunteer services and/or the distribution of information through the use of personal communication e.g. direct mailshot, telephone call or email. Those not previously contacted by the organisation are considered 'cold' contacts; 'warm' prospects are those who may have donated money or time in the past.

Donation

A gift of money, goods or time.

Donor

An individual or organisation giving a gift of money, goods or time.

Donor fatigue

Refers to a drop off in donor interest or income when the public appears to have reached saturation point with a particular cause or issue. Also refers to donors becoming immune to certain fundraising methods.

Donor's Charter

The Institute of Fundraising's Donor's Charter is a statement of principle setting out a fundraiser's commitment to donors. It states the standards a donor can expect from fundraisers and organisations before, during and after the processing of the gift.

Employee volunteering

The giving of time by staff to support charitable causes. Often supported by their employer through allowing time off, facilitating use of corporate resources or matching workplace fundraising.

Endowment

Funds designed to provide income for general or restricted use of an agency, institution or programme. An *expendable* endowment is a fund that must be invested to produce income. A *permanent* endowment is property (including land, buildings, cash or investments) that the trustees may not spend as if it were income. It must be held permanently, to be used to further the charity's purposes or produce an income for the charity.

Ethical fundraising

Refers to the ongoing dilemma of where a charity gets its money from, and the methods it uses. Charities have, for example, been criticised for receiving large donations from arms companies, baby milk manufacturers and companies involved in sweatshop labour in the developing world.

Excepted charities

Excepted charities, although required to comply with charity law, are not required to register with the Charity Commission. They can register voluntarily if they wish to do so. Examples include boy and girl scout charities, religious charities and armed forces charities.

Exempt charities

Charities that are exempt from the authority of the Charity Commission for England and Wales because they are considered to be adequately supervised by, or accountable to, some other body or authority. Examples include grant maintained schools and friendly societies.

Face-to-face fundraising
The practice of approaching people in the street or other public places to encourage them to sign up to a standing order or direct debit to support, or receive membership of, an organisation. The fundraiser may work for a professional fundraising organisation (PFO) employed by the organisation, or be part of the organisation's in-house team. See **Chuggers**

Fee income
Income from the sale of goods or services.

Fundraising consultant
A professional fundraiser who advises charities and other not-for-profit organisations on how to raise money.

Fundraising costs
Any expenditure aimed at generating donations, including payments to professional fundraising intermediaries.

Getting Britain Giving
A package of changes announced by the Chancellor in his 2000 Budget to increase charitable giving through new tax efficient methods. Incentives included lifting the £250 minimum limit for Gift Aid donations and a 10% government supplement on payroll donations.

Gift Aid
Scheme that allows charities to reclaim the tax paid on donations by UK taxpayers. For every £1 donated, the charity receives £1.28. Higher rate taxpayers can claim the difference between the higher rate of tax and the basic rate in their self assessment return.

Gifts in kind
Non-monetary donations to a charity or voluntary organisation. Can include the donation of computers from a company, or donations of company shares. Also refers to the donation of time, from a company or other body, to an organisation.

The Giving Campaign
National campaign launched in July 2001 with support from the voluntary sector and the government to raise the overall level of giving in the UK. Work during the three-year campaign focused on four areas: targeting wealthy people; tax-effective giving; employers and employees; and young people.

Grant
A sum of money given to a charity, organisation or individual, usually from some kind of grantmaking body, such as a charitable foundation or government department. A grant is different to a donation in that the recipient must usually meet specific criteria set by the grant maker about the target beneficiaries (e.g. minority ethnic groups or disadvantaged children) or geographical location (e.g. rural communities).

Institute of Fundraising
The professional body that seeks to represent all fundraisers. The Institute's mission is to develop, promote and champion excellence in fundraising. Activities include producing codes of fundraising practice and organising the annual National Convention.

Intern
An individual recruited by a charity or other organisation to work on a specific project or across departments for a limited period of time. Interns often receive a modest or token salary, but the internship gives them hands-on experience of working in the sector and of a particular cause or issue.

Legacy
A sum of money left to a charity or an organisation in a person's will, to be awarded when they die. It is estimated that legacies are worth around £1.5bn to the charity sector a year.

Legacy Promotion Campaign

A consortium of over 110 UK charities run through the Institute of Fundraising to increase the number of charitable bequests left in wills. The LPC's awareness-raising campaign, Remember a Charity, was launched in 2002.

Lottery distributors

Government bodies responsible for distributing a portion of money earned from the National Lottery to 'good causes'. Currently the Arts Councils, Sports Councils, Heritage Lottery Fund, New Opportunities Fund, Community Fund and Millennium Commission (grantmaking by the last three distributors will be taken over by a single distributor from 2005 – see **Big Lottery Fund**).

New Opportunities Fund

The body responsible for distributing National Lottery money to health, education and environment projects in the UK. An 'administrative merger' of the fund with the Community Fund in 2004 will eventually create a single body (see 'Big Lottery Fund').

National Lottery

UK-wide lottery launched in 1994 to raise money for 'good causes' as defined by parliament. Around 28p of every £1 spent on the National Lottery goes to good causes, which have received around £15bn to date. The remaining monies go to prize winners (50%); government lottery duty (12%); retailers commission (5%); operating costs (4.5%); and profit for Camelot, which runs the game (0.5%).

Non-governmental organisation (NGO)

A not-for-profit organisation, such as a charity, development organisation or environmental agency, which has an interest in making clear its independence from the government.

Not-for-profit

US-originated term for a charity or voluntary organisation.

Office of the Scottish Charity Regulator

OSCR is a Scottish Executive Agency and the regulator of charities in Scotland.

Online giving

Donating to a charity or other fundraising organisation via its website – or a generic website which handles donations for a number of charities – by entering credit card or bank details.

Payroll giving

A tax-effective method of employees giving to charity through their pay packet. Donations are deducted before tax, so each £1 given only costs the donor 78p (or 60p for higher rate tax payers). A valuable source of income for recipient organisations as donations are regular and often long term, enabling them to budget and plan ahead.

Personal solicitation

Method of fundraising involving speaking to donors in person. Includes door-to-door and street collections; face-to-face fundraising and presentations at events.

Professional fundraiser

A person involved in fundraising on behalf of a charity or other organisation.

Professional fundraising organisation (PFO)

A commercial organisation that promotes payroll giving on behalf of various charities. PFOs are paid a fee by the charity if workplace support is generated. Most PFOs belong to the Association of Professional Fundraising Organisations (APGPFO), which regulates their conduct.

Prospect
An individual, company or other organisation considered to be a potential source of financial support.

Public charitable collection
Activity involving volunteers or employees of a charity collecting cash donations on the street or door-to-door. Collectors carry and display a badge and certificate of authority.

Public Fundraising Regulatory Authority
The PFRA manages, promotes and advances public fundraising by personal solicitation, including face-to-face fundraising and house-to-house collections. It has an accreditation scheme for charities and professional fundraising organisations, and works with local authorities to help organise the allocation of sites for public fundraising.

Registered charity
An organisation with charitable purposes registered with the Charity Commission, with its legal status strictly governed by charity law. See **Charitable purpose**.

Reserves
Part of a charity's income funds that is freely available for its general purposes, once it has met its commitments and covered its planned expenditure.

Restricted funds
Funds donated to a charity that are subject to specific requirements which may be declared by the donor e.g. a donation to a cancer charity for breast cancer research. Funds may also be restricted by the fundraising organisation, for example for a specific appeal.

Share giving
A tax-effective method of giving to charity where individuals who donate shares are able to claim back full tax relief against the value of those shares.

Sponsored event
Fundraising activity where participants are sponsored to take part. Examples include fun runs and walks, cycle rides and countryside clear-ups.

Stakeholders
The individuals and/or groups involved in an organisation or project, including donors, beneficiaries and project funders.

Tax-effective giving
Method of donation where the charity and/or the donor can reclaim tax on gifts to charity. The core tax-effective giving methods are Gift Aid, payroll giving, share giving, gifts of land/property, legacies and charitable trusts.

Telephone fundraising
Use of telephone to encourage pledges or enquiries, or to promote an organisation through telemarketing conducted by an in-house team or external agency.

Third sector
Another term for the voluntary sector.

Trustee
A member of the governing board of a charity that is legally responsible for overall management and decision making within that organisation. S/he is obliged to act in the best interests of the charity and to ensure that it adheres to its charitable purposes. A trustee may be personally liable for the under-performance or illegal acts of a charity.

Voluntary and community sector (VCS)
Commonly used term to describe charities and other voluntary organisations in the UK.

Voluntary income
Grants, donations and other monies given freely to a fundraising organisation.

Volunteer
A person who gives without payment a portion of their time to an organisation as a worker or helper. The recipient organisation may compensate the volunteer for his or her travel or other expenses.